CW00470013

INSTAGRAM
FOR BUSINESS

BY SHAZ MEMON

INSTAGRAM FOR **BUSINESS**

BY SHAZ MEMON

This book has been published in 2020 by Verb Press.

Connect with Shaz Memon:

Website   shaz.co.uk
Instagram   instagram.com/shaz.memon
LinkedIn   linkedin.com/in/shazmemon

IN SUPPORT OF

The Instagram landscape is forever changing. I want to ensure that I can inform you of any future updates to this book.

Please scan the QR code or visit **instaforbusiness.co.uk/updates** to subscribe for free updates.

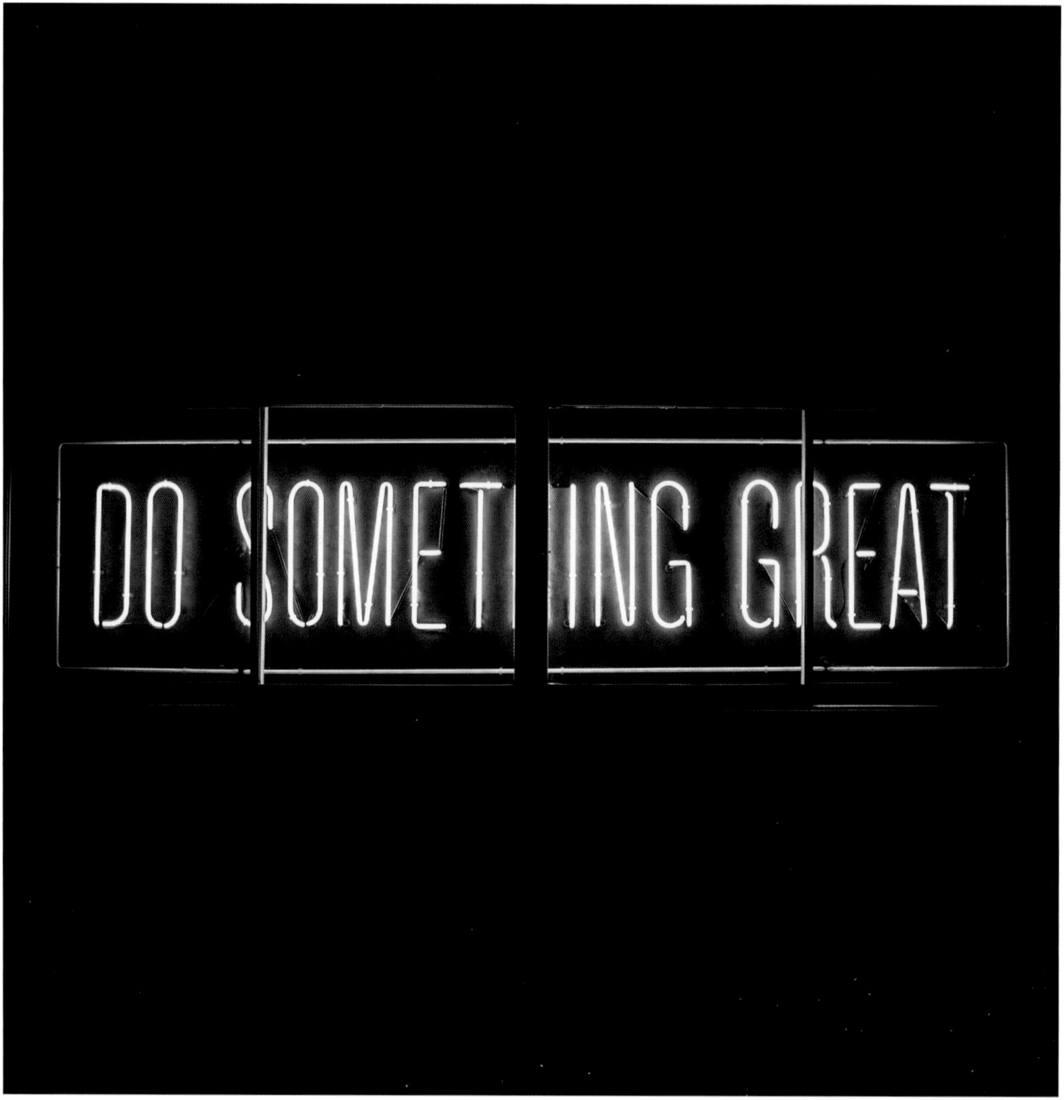
DO SOMETHING GREAT

Contents

A U T H O R

SHAZ / MEMON

Founder of Digimax

Founder of Wells on Wheels

Shaz Memon is the founder of Digimax in London. An astute business leader, designer and award-winning digital and dental marketing expert, Shaz has been featured in The Guardian, The Telegraph, The Daily Telegraph, The Sunday Telegraph, Huffington Post, MSN and Forbes.

WAKE ME UP WHEN I'M FAMOUS

Foreword

The world of social media can be overwhelming and intimidating – especially for those of us who remember the novelty of text messaging. The truth is, once mastered, social media can be an incredibly powerful platform for you and your business, offering exposure on a level that would have been inconceivable just 20 years ago.

At my agency, Digimax, we are often asked if we can manage Instagram accounts for our clients and personal brands, and the answer is always no. This is not because we do not welcome the work. Rather, we feel that the very best Instagram accounts are those that are real and genuine and managed by the people who know their business best – you and your team.

Instagram is not onerous at all and you don't need to be a celebrity or global brand to reap the benefits. This book is designed to help you grow your brand by harnessing the powers of online promotion – easily, successfully and with confidence.

I designed this book in a reference format to make learning easier. It allows you to skip to sections that are important to you, and learn using simple bite size information. I want to show any business, small or large, that Instagram is easy to master and a lot of fun too. I want you to be able to use Instagram to grow a brand effectively, creatively and confidently. Happy reading!

Wells on Wheels

Founded by Shaz Memon, Wells on Wheels helps families in rural regions of India. Women of all ages, including young girls, walk an average of 1-2 miles a day, carrying water on their heads from source back to their communities. Over time, the weight leads to chronic neck and back pain, with musculoskeletal disorders sometimes leading to complications during childbirth. Women may be pregnant or carrying a baby on their back in addition to their load. Young girls miss out on their childhood and don't get to attend school.

The Water Wheel is a large, round drum that is fitted with handles so it can be rolled along the ground with ease. These containers enable water collectors to roll liquid from wells rather than carry it on their heads. It can hold up to five times more water than a single bucket, reducing the number of trips needed and eliminating the burden on the head, back and neck.

10 percent of the proceeds from the sale of this book will go towards helping these women and girls (sometimes as young as seven years old), who must walk miles in the blazing heat to transport water to survive.

Let's ease the burden on our mothers, sisters and daughters.

One wheel costs £28 including logistics. I hope this book helps you as much as your purchase helps us to provide Wells on Wheels to those who need it most.

Learn more about Wells on Wheels by visiting: **www.wellsonwheels.co.uk**

wells on wheels

wells.on.wheels
Maharashtra, India

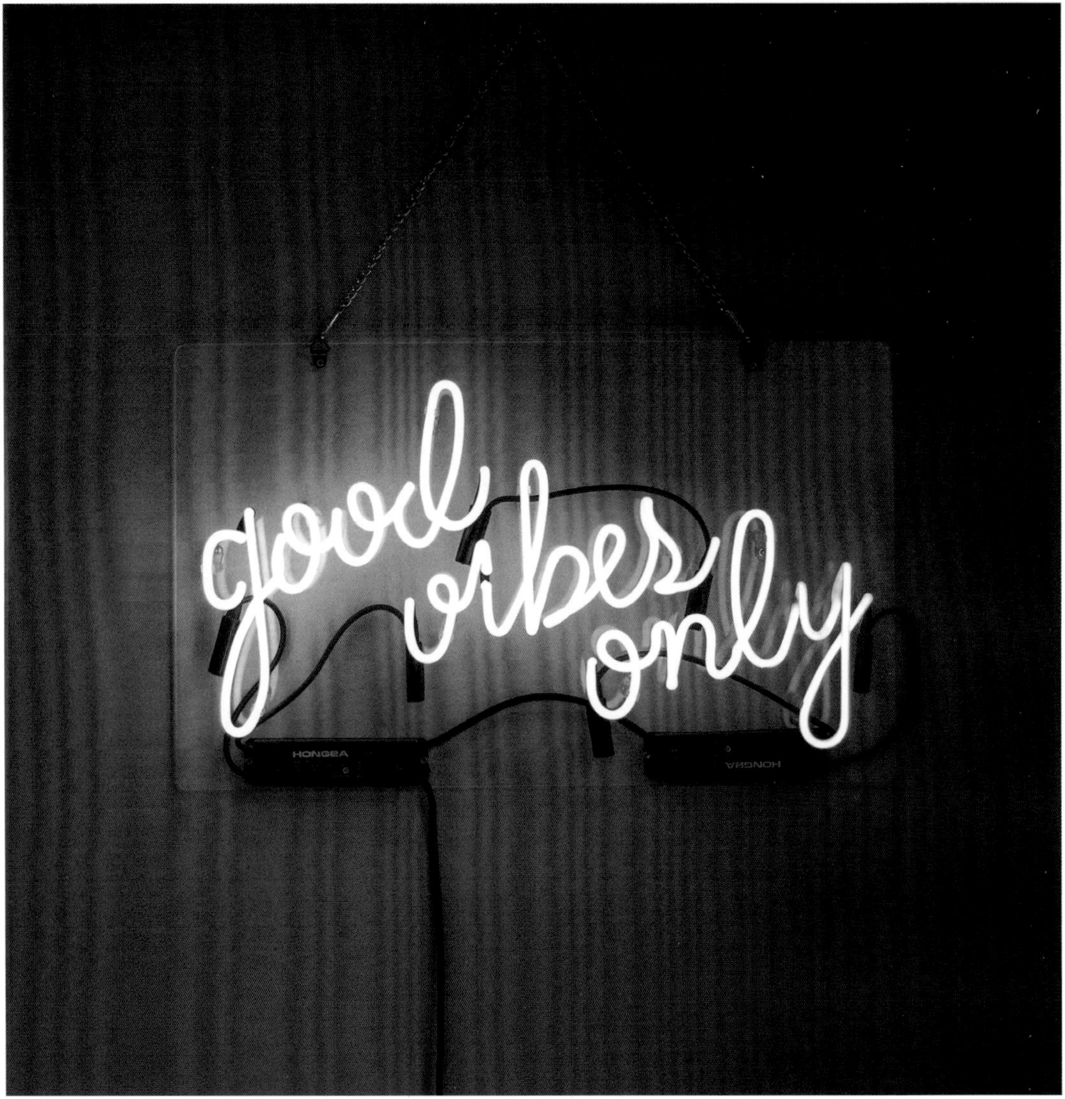
good vibes only

Mental health

We cannot, of course, discuss the merits and commercial benefits of social media without making reference to the effect it can have on our mental health.

In a highly connected digital world, social media has become an enormous force in all of our lives. It enables us to engage and communicate with almost anyone around the globe at any given time and, whilst this has been revolutionary in terms of both social and business interactions, it's not without its downfalls.

This book has been written to celebrate Instagram as an effective marketing tool and a fun way to engage with potential customers. I encourage you to enjoy to the full what it has to offer in terms of raising your profile and awareness of the importance of what your business has to offer. However, I do feel it is just as important to understand that it can also seem a bit of a minefield – at times, it may knock our confidence as much as it boosts business.

There is a whole raft of research to suggest that social media has strong links to mental health issues – in particular, when overused or without us remaining mindful of its potential dark side. The negative effects on self-esteem have, in turn, been linked to higher rates of depression, anxiety, loneliness, envy, narcissism and even decreased social skills.

Naturally, we all have our fair share of insecurities, but even the most confident and outgoing among us can be affected by anonymous and thoughtless remarks made online...

Continued on page 242

Introduction

Finding a voice within the noisy world of social media can prove challenging for SME'S looking to maximise their online presence. This brave new digital world offers an abundance of platforms to market services and products and create an online presence to build a brand.

Indeed, it is the active, engaging and inspiring Instagram accounts that catch the eye, provoke interest, build brands and generate new clients.

Founded in 2010, Instagram, has taken the world by storm with statistics evidencing 500-plus million daily users and one billion plus monthly active users. A mostly photo- and video-sharing platform, it is a powerful marketing tool and is perfectly placed to showcase the services you have to offer and the quality of your products in exciting and very visual ways.

Too often, people are daunted by the prospect of managing their own Instagram account and resort to outsourcing to a third party, believing it to be a time-saving and easier option. But authenticity counts for everything and your followers will expect meaningful and genuine interactions with the 'real deal' i.e. you. Whilst there is nothing fundamentally wrong with using an agency to manage your social media, nobody knows your customer base better than you and your team. Once you've got to grips with the basics, the management of your own Instagram profile will give followers a far more honest account of who you are and what your company has to offer, far better than anyone else can. You'll also find it takes a lot less time to manage than you thought.

What is Instagram?

Instagram (also known as IG or Insta) is a Facebook owned social media networking app that allows users to upload and share photos and videos to other users, platforms and social networks. Created by Kevin Systrom and Mike Krieger, it was launched in 2010 exclusively on iOS. Co-founder Kevin Systrom says he has no regrets about selling Instagram to Facebook for $1 billion even though it is now worth 100 times that.

The ability to snap, share and edit photos on the go is at the heart of Instagram's success. Indeed, it has built a devout community based on a single idea: the capturing and sharing of beautiful images. You only have to spend 10 minutes on the app scrolling through a multitude of feeds to be hooked. We already knew that a picture is worth a thousand words; Instagram knows it is worth a lot more. By embodying a cultural shift towards photo inboxes, it has enabled people to connect via imagery, throwing off the shackles of complex social relations.

On Instagram, the imagery stands alone and speaks for itself – loudly and proudly. The ability to add filters turns the flattest, coldest picture into picturesque, hazy and sun-kissed dreams filled with emotion. Instagram is a whole new world where images and video, rather than text-based content, reign supreme.

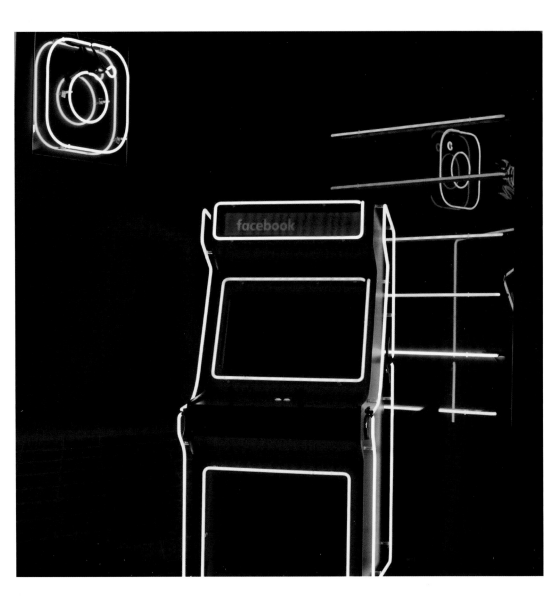

Instagram vs Facebook

With so many different social media platforms to choose from, it can be a minefield deciding which to use to best promote your brand. Facebook and Instagram are widely considered important marketing platforms.

Whilst Facebook might well provide the initial online encounter with potential customers and clients, Instagram offers key support in building this awareness and enhancing on-going consumer relationships. Very often, Instagram is the 'go to' space for those looking for fast and easy engagement. Scrolling through their Instagram feed, they can get a taste of day-to-day life at your business via high quality images, candid posts, new case studies, team profiles and product updates.

Instagram also leans towards a more savvy and digitally inclined demographic, opening up a plethora of marketing opportunities at the touch of a button to an audience who live on their phones and laptops.

500 million
accounts are active
every day

1 billion
accounts are active
every month

400 million
accounts use Instagram
Stories every day

27 million
business accounts
in existence

80%
of users follow a
business account

30%
of users bought
something they
discovered
on Instagram

25%
of Instagram ads
are videos

53%
of users are aged
between 18-29

25%
of users are aged
between 30-49

Making **Millennials** and **Gen X** the largest generations using the platform

If you are using Instagram for the first time

When using any form of digital technology for the first time, especially to promote a brand or business, it's understandable to be a little reticent to dive in headfirst. I recommend simply downloading the app and spending a week or two browsing through it before forging ahead.

Familiarisation with the interface is a really good way to ease yourself into the learning. Taking the time to peruse other accounts, especially those within your industry, can give you a better idea of what to post – and you may even get some inspiration for style and content along the way.

Don't get bogged down with trying to build followers from day one. Take time to get to know the app and the rest will follow.

Getting started on Instagram is quick, easy and can be done from your smartphone or computer. **See pages 30-33 on Creating your account.**

Keeping it real

There's a good reason why Instagram is so popular and why it has become the world's fastest growing social media platform. Quite simply, it allows users to interact with real content. Whilst the more traditional methods of advertising and promoting remain effective, we are all now very much tuned into personal recommendations – and the internet supports this. We value genuine word-of-mouth testimonials, real-life feedback and endorsements by way of online rating systems – all of which support the use of social media to increase brand visibility.

To this end, Instagram is not very 'corporate'. The accounts that offer real visual insights into a person or business tend to be the most successful, because they share genuine and personal glimpses into their world. Often, the owners of these accounts speak their followers' language so that it feels as if the content is coming directly from the individual rather than a room full of marketing executives. As long as you stay true to yourself when posting content, you have a much greater chance of engaging with potential customers organically and positively.

We must always remember to 'keep it real'. Your Instagram voice will need to match your real-life persona and brand ethos so that when online followers become new customers, they already know what to expect. This friendliness and familiarity can quickly turn new customers into repeat customers.

GETTING STARTED

Creating your account from the app

Creating an account on Instagram is incredibly easy and, because it is designed as a mobile app, the best place to start is with your mobile phone. All you need to get going is a smartphone and an email address and/or phone number.

1. First you will need to download the app. If you are using an iPhone, this can be done from the app store. If you're on Android, head over to the Google Play store and search for 'Instagram'.

2. Once installed, click on the **Instagram** icon to open it.

3. If using an iPhone tap on **Create New Account**. For Android users, tap on **Sign up with email or phone number**. Follow the instructions on screen and enter in your details.

4. Next you'll need to create a username and password. **See page 56 on Picking a name.**

5. Lastly, you'll be directed to fill out your profile info. **See page 55 on Writing your bio.**

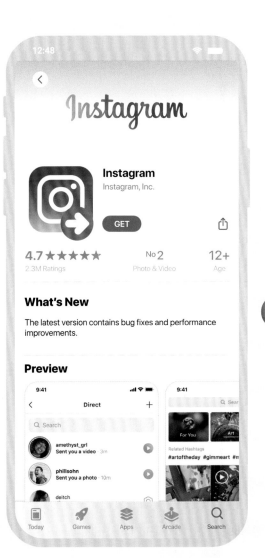

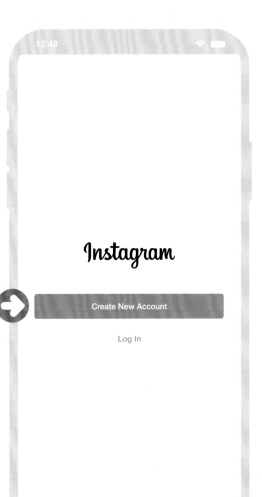

Instagram

Sign up to see photos and videos from your friends.

 f Log in with Facebook

OR

 Mobile Number or Email

Full Name

Username

Password

Sign Up

By signing up, you agree to our Terms, Data Policy and Cookies Policy.

Have an account? Log in

Get the app.

Creating your account from a computer

If you prefer to work from your computer or laptop, it is just as easy to set up an Instagram account.

1. Open your web browser and go to **www.instagram.com**

2. Enter your details, choose a username (**See page 56 on Pick a name**) and click **Next**, or if you want to use your Facebook account to log in, click **Log in with Facebook**.

3. Follow the steps presented to you which will vary depending on your registration method.

4. Lastly, you'll be directed to fill out your profile info. **See page 55 on Writing your bio.**

Understanding your icons

1 **Story Camera**
Add photos and videos to your Story.

2 **IGTV**
Here you can view videos from the people you follow and popular 'creators'.

3 **Direct Messages**
The paper plane icon represents your direct messages. A number above the icon means you have a new direct message.

4 **Three Dots**

Report	Report a post to Instagram
Mute	Mute an account's posts, an alternative to unfollowing
Unfollow	You will no longer see an account's content in your feed
Copy Link	Copies the posts hyperlink, so you can paste it elsewhere
Share to...	Easy sharing to other platforms such as on WhatsApp
Turn on Post Notifications	Get notified each time an account posts

5 **Heart**
'Hearting' a post shows you like it. Instagram uses this to serve you other similar accounts and posts you may also like.

6 **Comment**
Here you can comment on a post.

7 **Share Post**
The paper icon allows you to share a post to one or more people.

1

Instagram

2

3

shaz.memon

•••

4

INSTAGRAM
FOR **BUSINESS**

BY SHAZ MEMON

5

6

7

309 Likes

shaz.memon Instagram for Business *OUT NOW!

6 MINUTES AGO ·

Instagram

 shaz.memon   •••

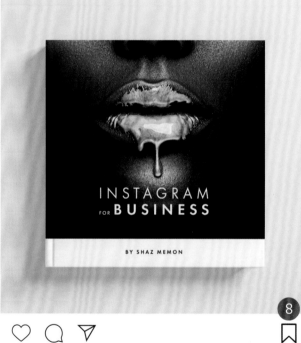

309 Likes

shaz.memon Instagram for Business *OUT NOW!

6 MINUTES AGO

Understanding your icons continued

Bookmark
Save a post to review later.

Home
Home shows a feed of photos posted by you and people you follow.

Search and Explore
Here you can search for other Instagram accounts you might like.

Post Camera
Upload or take photos and videos within the Instagram app, and share them on your feed.

Activity Heart
See new followers, comments, likes, tags and account suggestions here.

My Profile
See your own feed by clicking on your profile icon/image.

How to like a post

To like or 'heart' a post, press the heart icon beneath a post or double tap the picture in the post.

This notifies the creator, as well as helps Instagram serve tailored suggestions to you for other posts you may also like.

Tap the heart icon to like a post or double tap the picture in a post

Instagram is testing hiding likes

Instagram is known for its 'likes' count but, in recent times, the platform has received a lot of bad press about the narcissistic nature of orchestrated posts designed to attain likes and the implicit and detrimental links with mental health.

At the time of writing this book, Instagram has been testing out removing and hiding likes in Australia, Brazil, Canada, Ireland, Italy, Japan, and New Zealand.

Instagram head Adam Mosseri claims the move to hide likes (you can see your tally but not those of other accounts) is to reduce anxiety and stress on users – 'The idea is to try to depressurise Instagram, make it less of a competition and give people more space to focus on connecting with people they love and things that inspire them.'

This has been welcomed by many around the world, but there has been some pushback from users. An argument remains that hiding engagement metrics will make it harder to determine whose follower count is legitimate and who really has 'influence'.

Heartbreaker

What do I do with my existing account?

If you enjoy using Instagram already and feel that going 'professional' might take away the fun of being able to post what you like to your friends without giving too much thought to it, then I suggest you split your identities. Make your current Instagram account private (**See page 47 on Privacy**) and create a second professional identity that is not set to private.

Instagram allows you to have more than one account (**See page 44 on Creating an additional account**). I would also advise renaming the identity you decide to keep private - to one that will not be easily found by customers.

If you don't like the idea of having more than one account, then I suggest archiving posts that don't match the brand you are trying to build (**See page 113 on Archiving posts**) and only using your account for posts and stories that match your defined identity (**See page 89 on What is your voice?**). A photo of you passed out drunk on the pavement with your friends posing alongside paramedics may not be 'on brand'.

Creating an additional account

If you're the Bruce Wayne of your industry and already have an account that you want or need to keep separate from your private life, the good news is you can simply create another one. It's easy to generate an additional account and Instagram allows you to switch between multiple accounts at the touch of a button.

From your Instagram profile screen, click on your profile image on the bottom right-hand side and click the little black down arrow next to your account name at the top of the app. Click the **+ Add account** button and follow the steps.

To switch between accounts, simply click on the down arrow again and this will bring up the other account/s you have. Click on the relevant profile to assume your identity.

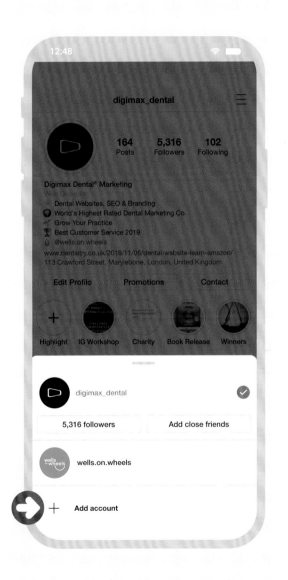

digimax_dental

164
Posts

5,316
Followers

102
Following

Digimax Dental® Marketing

Dental Websites, SEO & Branding
World's Highest Rated Dental Marketing Co.
Grow Your Practice
Best Customer Service 2019
@wells.on.wheels
www.dentistry.co.uk/2019/11/06/dental-website-learn-amazon/
113 Crawford Street, Marylebone, London, United Kingdom

Edit Profile   Promotions   Contact

Highlight   IG Workshop   Charity   Book Release   Winners

digimax_dental

5,316 followers   Add close friends

wells.on.wheels

+   Add account

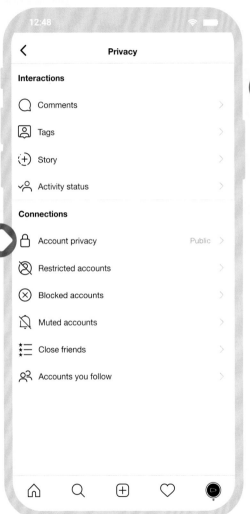

Privacy

Interactions

Comments

Tags

Story

Activity status

Connections

Account privacy   Public

Restricted accounts

Blocked accounts

Muted accounts

Close friends

Accounts you follow

Account privacy

Private account

When your account is private, only people you approve can see your photos and videos on Instagram. Your existing followers won't be affected. Learn More.

Privacy

For your business and brand, you obviously want potential customers to be able to find you, so make sure you keep the settings to public. Business accounts are public by default. Should you have a pre-existing account (personal or hobby) that you wish to retain for use with friends and hide from followers, then read on.

When setting up your profile, Instagram makes everything public by default. You can set your account to private so that followers have to be approved by you before they can see what you share. Only these approved followers will be able to see your photos and videos.

Changing your privacy preferences is simple – just click on your profile icon at the bottom and then onto the menu in the top right-hand corner. Click **Settings > Privacy > Account privacy.** Then toggle the **Private account** switch to the 'on' state.

Upgrading to a business profile

The next step is to decide whether to keep your account as a personal account (which is the Instagram default) or upgrade to a business profile. My advice? Upgrade. With a business profile, you have access to detailed, analytical data and additional tools that you don't get with a personal account, ultimately giving you more control over your marketing objectives.

'Instagram Insights' is a fantastic feature (**See page 163 on Analysing your audience**), giving you information on visitor demographics and engagement, such as gender, age, location and times of day your followers are most active. This tool allows you to then analyse what does and doesn't work so that you can tailor future posts based on your most popular content, saving you time and effort down the line.

Also, not only does a business account allow you to include a clickable location address in your profile to make it easy for potential customers to locate you, it also offers the option to categorise yourself within your chosen industry.

To upgrade, click on your profile icon at the bottom and then onto the menu in the top right-hand corner. Click **Settings > Account > Switch to Business Account**. Then click the **Switch to Business** button that appears. Once upgraded, click on the **Edit Profile** button at any time to update any aspects of your profile, including **Contact options**.

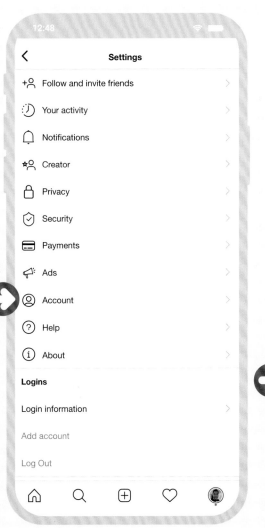

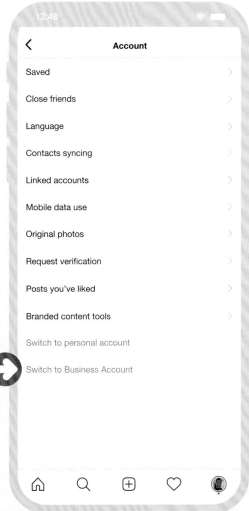

Personal or business branding?

Deciding who or what you are promoting on Instagram should be your first step. Is this account for you as the face of the company or an account to represent the whole business and brand? It's perfectly acceptable to brand yourself (**See page 171 on Personal branding**), and in some cases may even encourage greater engagement with your followers. Besides, you might only be in the early stages of your business, or you may have a personal brand development plan, in which case a personally branded professional Instagram profile may be the best way forward for now.

However, if your business is well established and you have a great range of products or services you are looking to promote, then focus on this. You can still add personal imagery and stories, but the predominant messaging should focus on the business as a whole.

If you can't decide which way to go, or if you want to promote both your brand and yourself, then simply follow the steps on **page 44 on Creating an additional account**. You might find that each account attracts different followers, which you can use to your advantage by sharing posts and stories between the two.

Your profile photo or logo?

When someone visits your Instagram account, your profile picture is one of the first things you are judged on. Think about your overall brand. If you are promoting yourself, then a clear professional, friendly headshot is a good start. Just make sure the aesthetics of your profile picture match that of your feed.

Keep your backgrounds neutral, uncluttered and up-to-date. A festive photo won't look great come June so avoid using time-sensitive images. Visitors will think you only use Instagram intermittently and may be less inclined to get in touch.

If your profile is centred on your business, then using your logo for your profile picture is the best option. This is brand reinforcement from the get-go, which will help with long-term brand recognition and show visitors what it is you have to offer.

Your graphic designer will be able to send you an Instagram-friendly version of your logo.

12:48

digimax_dental ☰

164
Posts

5,316
Followers

102
Following

Digimax Dental® Marketing
Web Designer
⚡ Dental Websites, SEO & Branding
🌐 World's Highest Rated Dental Marketing Co.
🌱 Grow Your Practice
🏆 Best Customer Service 2019
💧 @wells.on.wheels
www.dentistry.co.uk/2019/11/06/dental-website-learn-amazon/
113 Crawford Street, Marylebone, London, United Kingdom

| Edit Profile | Promotions | Contact |

+				
Highlight	IG Workshop	Charity	Book Release	Winners

Writing your bio

A study has shown that it takes less than two-tenths of a second for a visitor on Instagram to form their first impression of you, so make sure yours is a positive one!

It sounds obvious, but make sure your products/services are included in your bio. Instagram limits the number of characters and lines you can use, so choose wisely.

Instagram only allows one website address link for promotion, so use it to direct potential customers to the page you wish them to see at any given moment. This can be changed whenever you choose. It may be to a page on your website, a booking link or even an external website. You can also direct traffic in posts by mentioning the link in your bio – for example: 'Our new Spring collection is here. Check it out. See link in bio.'

If you've created your own branded hashtag (**See page 145 on Your own hashtag**) then this should definitely be included, as well as any other keywords that help sell your brand and define who you are. Whilst you should be professional with what you write, don't be afraid to show a bit of personality.

It is easier and quicker for visitors to perceive information in smaller, bite-size pieces, so consider breaking up the information in your bio with line spacing. You can also enhance it with emojis to add some colour and humour to your profile. They can work like bullet points whilst giving your brand a friendly 'face'.

I have refrained from providing an example of the perfect brand bio, as this will be personal to each business or individual. Seek inspiration from other profiles to create a bio that is fitting to your brand.

To personalise your bio, click on the **Edit Profile** button.

Pick a name

If you've chosen to use Instagram to promote your business rather than yourself, it's always a good idea to include your company name and, where possible, your location – for example @**BobsButchersHammersmith.** Showing a location in your profile name is a great way of encouraging local engagement. When you like the post of another local business, influencer or potential customer, they will immediately see you are local to them and will be more likely to check out your account.

If you have multiple locations, or if your services and products are available nationwide and not just locally, then aim to use just your company name.

If your preferred username has already been taken, don't simply add numbers at the end – unless they are directly relevant to your brand, of course. Adding numbers can affect your credibility as a business and may suggest the account is not genuine; besides, if someone else has your preferred name, why would you want to risk getting confused with their account? So think of something different and unique to ensure you stand out.

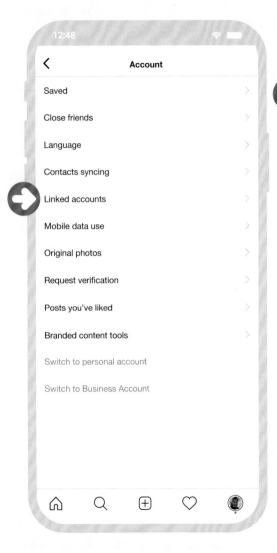

Connecting your Instagram account to Facebook

There are many benefits to connecting your accounts, including building brand awareness and reaching a wider audience.

Once connected, you can choose to share your stories and posts to Facebook. This means you can use one post to reach followers on both platforms at once. But don't do this too often. Be mindful of the fact that you may have the same followers on both platforms so be sure to retain new fresh and original content for both to avoid repetition fatigue. If you share something to Facebook that you later realise you didn't intend to – you can always head over to Facebook and to delete the post.

From your Instagram account, click on your profile icon and then onto the menu in the top right-hand corner. Click **Settings > Account > Linked accounts > Facebook**. Then click **Continue** when asked 'Instagram' Wants to Use 'facebook.com' to Sign In. Follow the prompts to finish connecting your Facebook account.

Embedding an Instagram feed on your website

Adding your Instagram feed to your website is a great way to keep it fresh and current. Once built, most websites do not change much in content except when updating blogs or if there are new team members or new products and services to add or delete. This makes it hard for potential customers to gauge how current the information is. By linking your Instagram feed, not only are you providing up-to-date and engaging content, but also encouraging your website visitors to follow you on Instagram.

Adding your Instagram feed to your website can be done by using code directly from Instagram. Visit **www.instagram.com/developer/embedding** to learn more. If you are not hands-on with making changes to your website, get your website designer involved.

Alternatively, there are a number of free and paid-for tools that can do this for you, such as **Smash Balloon** and **Juicer**. Again, consult your website designer.

Follow us

FINDING AND FOLLOWING

Syncing your phone contact list

You can connect your phone's contacts to Instagram, which will then show you a list of those with an Instagram account. From there, you can choose who to follow.

Click on your profile icon and then onto the menu in the top right-hand corner. Click **Discover people > Connect contacts > Connect > Allow Access**. You can now tap on **Follow** next to the contacts you would like to follow.

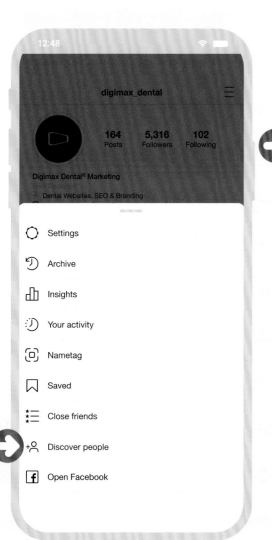

Following accounts, people and hashtags

Now that you're all set up, it's time to search for businesses, individuals or topics related to your profession. Look for brands you work with, people you may have provided your services to, or who use your products. Look for those who have a large number of followers on Instagram, including influencers and motivational speakers from your field, and start building your network. Be aware that who you choose to follow is publicly available for others to see. Following a reasonable number of accounts adds to the authenticity of your account when customers come to view your profile. Not only does it show that you're engaging and active on Instagram, but the type of accounts you follow is also an indicator of your personality.

When you're looking for new accounts or people to follow, simply click on the little magnifying glass at the bottom of the app, and type in the person or business name you're looking for. Click on their account and hit **Follow**. Sometimes you may find three or four accounts with similar names, so do double-check their profile to ensure you're following who you meant to and not just someone with a similar name.

Stay abreast of current trends and topics. Following popular hashtags is a great way to build a brand and extend your reach. Keep an eye out for what hashtags your peers are using and regularly check in on popular, industry-relevant tags. This is very simple to do. Use the search bar as you would if you were looking for a person, but choose a relevant term, such as 'new home' if you're an estate agent, or 'balayage' if you're a hairdresser. Click on the heading **Tags** and search through all the different hashtags relating to this term. You can even follow hashtags now and the top posts each week for that tag will appear in your feed. **See page 134 on Embrace those hashtags**.

Who should you follow back?

If you're starting on your Instagram journey, it can be tempting to follow back everyone who follows you – it's only polite, isn't it? Well, actually no. For a start, Instagram has a cap of 7,500 accounts you can follow, so only select accounts you wish to support or with content you want to see. Tread carefully as a number of your followers may be following you just to get you to follow back, thereby inflating their figures and 'evidence' of their popularity.

These are not always real organic followers, so check their feeds before reciprocating. Are they a potential customer? Do they live in the same country as you? Could they influence their followers for your brand or service or is there a mutual, viable business reason to follow them back? The keyword here is mutual. If you each have content that is meaningful to each other, then, by all means follow them back – but be selective. If their feed is full of questionable content, then ignore. Your brand reputation will be judged on the people with whom you engage, so make sure you choose wisely.

Use this genuine follow-back trick

The following method was used by my team for a popular high street brand to grow its follower base by 400%.

Start by finding Instagram accounts that already interact with your target audience, such as local shops, spas, restaurants, cab firms, local solicitors and points of interest and so on. Click on their list of followers. Do this by clicking on **Following** at the top of their profile. Go to each follower's profile and like a few of their pictures. The account owners will receive a notification letting them know you liked their photo. Some profiles may be private, so you can skip those.

It's human nature to check out who liked your post, particularly if it is from a location you recognise (**See page 56 on Pick a name**). If the account owner is interested in your account, they will follow you back. This little trick can help to gain thousands of real followers who may be interested in your product or service. Naturally, this will require time investment from your side, but it works!

Please do not do this with competitor businesses. It's not cool and just encourages them to do them same to you once they realise, which means a slippery slope for ethical practices! #keepitethical

Do not mass follow

There is a belief that following lots of accounts is one way to gain followers. Mass following doesn't help you in the long term and isn't likely to help you gain followers that are genuinely interested in your account.

The people you follow reflect on you and your brand. If you're following thousands of accounts, you run the risk of missing content from those who matter and accounts with whom engagement could mean a boost for your brand.

Seeing an account that follows thousands of accounts is a turn-off for proficient Instagram users as it can make you look a bit spammy and desperate.

Do not buy followers

Somewhere along your Instagram journey, an opportunity to 'buy followers' may present itself. Building an Instagram following takes time so it can be tempting to cheat the process in this way. Please don't.

Not only is it disingenuous, but you'll also be going against Instagram's Terms of Use. Should you choose to take a shortcut, you run the risk of a ban from the platform.

Moreover, this lack of integrity can be very damaging to your brand and reputation in the long run. High follower numbers but low engagement are obvious signs that you may have bought your followers, and if potential customers see that you're trying to pull the wool over their eyes, they may think twice about your professionalism and overall work ethic.

WHAT TO POST

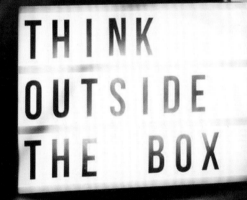

Happy Smiling Customers	Team Photo	Case Study or Product Shot
Location Imagery	MD or Founder Photo	Charity Work
Team Event	Client Gift	Technology

Power of 9

We all know that first impressions count. Whether it's your physical appearance (clean shoes, nice smile and tidy hair) or your website homepage (engaging imagery, clear messaging and concise text) that first look or initial visit is key. Your Instagram profile is no different. In fact, with Instagram the attention span is far lower and visitors need to be hooked from the moment they lay eyes on your page, which means your account is likely to be judged on the first nine squares they see, what I like to call 'The Power of 9'.

The first 9 squares say a lot about you and your brand and – if you want visitors to scroll further down – at least 75% of these images should be telling your story. If your first nine squares are all pictures of your dog, then this is not representing the professional you.

Always be conscious of the overall story those 9 squares are telling. Do they epitomise you, your brand and your offering in such a way that will make people want to scroll down to see more? Think of these 9 squares as your book cover – how would you like to be judged?

This hit home when I found one Christmas that our first 9 squares on our Digimax Instagram account were full of pictures of gifts and hampers we received from clients. I am sure it looked great to some, but many people visiting our Instagram for the first time would have disengaged as they wouldn't have seen how amazing and powerful our websites are and how we are bespoke in our approach to branding and creating identities for clients within niche industries. We corrected this immediately.

Define the type of customer you want most

What exactly are you hoping to achieve from Instagram? Do your followers know exactly who you are and what you're offering? If you're service based, chances are you have a range of offerings or packages with differing price points to best suit your client's needs. Or, perhaps, you appeal to a particular audience but wish to broaden your scope? Make sure you create posts based on the type of work you want and use this as your standard when choosing content.

For example, if you are a beauty therapist seeking to get more dermatology clients in the chair, then share stories of successful skin treatment journeys or feature fact-file type posts on the importance of a healthy, regular cleansing routine and how to make a great first impression.

Start by making a list of the services you offer. Which are the ones you want to promote the most? Is this consistently clear across your posts? If you own a car repair business and specialise in vehicle wrapping and graphics, is this immediately apparent? There's no point pushing your MOT services when what you really want is to be pimping rides. You cannot get the type of work you want if you don't define it, so design your posts to direct clients to these services.

Tell people what they don't know

People don't know what they don't know – and they will continue to not know until you tell them! If you have a large multicultural team who between them speak more than 10 languages, have won an award for customer service, or even if you have an office dog that greets all customers with a smile, then share it on your Instagram account.

Never assume that people will know key facts about you just because the information is on your website. The truth is, they may never get as far as that. Instagram might be the first time they've ever seen or heard of you, so think of all the things that make you and your brand unique to entice them to look further.

Post inspiration

Events
Anniversaries and company milestones

Birthdays
Team member birthdays

Training
On-site and off-site team training

People
Team photos. Posts with a face get 38% more likes

New
Showcase anything interesting that is new with your brand

Case Studies
Completed projects or work that you're proud to show off

Gratitude
Gifts and thank you cards. Tag gifts with permission

Wins
Finalist logos and award wins or accreditations

Advice
Interesting top tips with your own angle

Sneak Peek
Behind the scenes peek into any exciting developments

Local Events
Share any fun events you are part of in your local community.

Tutorials
Team training, on-site and off-site

Brands
Showcase brands you work with and use

Inspiration
Anything that inspires you

Surroundings
Let followers know how beautiful your location is

Prizes
Offer a prize to the winner of a poll or quiz on your 'Gram'

Reposts
Reposts from fans. Easily done by screenshotting their post

Your Why
Share your 'why' with your audience

Capturing gifts

Chances are you've built up great relationships with your clients or customers and you may be no stranger to receiving a gift or two.

Take the opportunity to ask them if they mind you taking a picture of the gift along with someone in the team receiving it. Alternatively, you can take a picture of your gifts and post them on your stories **See page 214 on Instagram Stories**. If the 'thank you' gesture is particularly photo-worthy, then share it on your feed as a more permanent post. Alternatively, share it in your Stories. If you want to tag your gifter in the post, remember to ask for their permission first.

What is your voice?

They say a picture tells a thousand words, and so with every image you post on Instagram, you need to ensure the words tell your story succinctly. Don't post simply for the sake of posting – this just litters your account with random noise. Take time to ensure every post has a clearly defined purpose.

The captions and information you provide with the images you share should work seamlessly to convince a follower (or any potential customer) to continue enjoying your posts in their feed and, ultimately, buy from or work with you. At Digimax, we receive many referrals from people who have never been clients but who have seen our posts or Stories and liked them. The power of your brand may even bring you referrals from people who have yet to buy into your services themselves.

The key is consistency – in tone of voice, quality of your images and colour palette. Images with a recognisable brand identity give followers a visual signal. Similarly, the tone of your captions needs to remain the same on every post to ensure followers recognise your voice, know who you are and understand what you stand for.

Who even are you?

Does your online persona reflect who you are in real life? Are you representing the truest version of yourself in your social media activity? For example, if one of your USPs is that your products are eco-friendly and sustainably sourced, does your chosen imagery illustrate this? Is this ethos reflected in your business environment? Are your team known for their helpful and friendly personalities? Do you have images showing them smiling with happy customers?

Your Instagram account should be able to convey all of this without potential customers having to hunt for the answer. The most successful influencers I know are those whose online and real-life persona match. What are the attributes that define you and what are those you wish to communicate to your followers? Use these as the foundations for every post.

Be interesting

Professionalism is key when it comes to your brand's Instagram account. The type of content you post should differ to content you share on your personal account but need not be dry or dull - nor does every image need to be directly product or service related. If your business is in cake making, it doesn't mean that every single post should be of your finished cakes, no matter how delicious looking they are. Mix it up (no pun intended!) by giving your followers a glimpse of the process. How do you make your frosting and toppings? What does your kitchen looks like? Do you buy any of your ingredients, such as fresh fruit, from a local business?

Choose images that show off your personality, reinforce your brand identity and showcase your offerings. Showing off your work environment and sharing photos of a happy team are just as important as sharing pictures of your finished projects or new products. **See pages 84 and 85 for post inspiration.**

Cool Instagram layouts

I often get asked how some accounts have been able to neatly keep certain style posts aligned to one side of the grid or have a clear structure on the order in which their posts appear.

If you want to have that level of control, that is great and, if you have the time to do this, even better. However, my advice is to not get fixated on this at the cost of getting any posts out. Having another thing to do that prevents you from uploading regularly is not productive for a little bit of beautification!

If you're looking for an easy option, then check out an app called **Preview**, which makes creating layouts easy.

What makes a good post?

There are several factors that need to be considered to make sure you are uploading quality posts. As Instagram is a photo-sharing platform, the most obvious is imagery. Good quality, well-framed and nicely lit images, that grab the attention of followers as they scroll, are key. There's no point having a killer caption if the image is an out of focus and poorly lit product shot.

However, if your image is spot on, then back it up with a well thought out and engaging caption. Short titles and key phrases associated with the image you're sharing will help the viewer remember you. Ask questions in your caption to encourage engagement. Comments spark conversations and, ultimately, raise brand awareness.

Most importantly, remember to check spelling. Nothing is more off-putting for a business than poor spelling, grammar and punctuation. You are, after all, promoting a professional service or product.

What times to post?

The best time to post on Instagram can vary widely. Every Instagram account has a unique audience, which means it's important to work out what time works best for you.

One factor to take into consideration are people's work hours – most don't have bosses who allow them to spend the day on social media, so aim for lunchtimes and evenings where possible.

There are a many online tools to help you work out the optimum posting times for your particular country, but you can also get a good idea yourself by using Instagram's native analytics tool – Instagram Insights (**See page 163 on Analysing your audience**). Not only does this tool tell you where your followers are located, their gender and age, but most importantly when they're most active on Instagram, allowing you to plan your uploads around these key times.

How often should you post?

Just as it's important to know when to post on Instagram, it's also key to know how often to post.

Higher frequency doesn't necessarily equate to higher engagement, but it does depend on your offering and reach. One particular fashion brand posts up to 30 times a day, but they have 10.8 million followers around the globe, so these frequent postings ensure they see at least one or two of these posts at any given time during the day. But a fashion brand tends to have plenty of new content/clothes for every post, which means it doesn't get too repetitive. If you are marketing to a small and select local audience, 30 posts of visually similar images a day will annoy followers and is likely to be hard to maintain.

According to a Union Metrics study, brands post on average 1.5 times a day. This is a good rate for most businesses and a realistic goal in terms of keeping content fresh and varied.

The key is to work out realistically how often you think you can post and how much interesting and varied content you have. Don't post simply for the sake of posting something – uploading a poor image will do you more harm than not posting at all. My advice would be to post a minimum of once a week, but to be extremely regular with your Instagram stories (**See page 214 on Instagram Stories**). You can go daily or multiple times a week with stories.

+

MONTHLY TIP

PLAN SMART.

FILL OUT YOUR
WEEKLY AGENDA
NOTING WHEN YOU
WILL DO WHAT AND
HOW. THIS WILL
KEEP YOU ON TRACK
TO ATTAINING YOUR
GOAL.

NOTES

IMPORTANT DATES

JAN   FEB   MAR

SUNDAY   MONDAY

Strike a balance

Finding the right balance to your pictures is key. Just because you are a baker or a butcher doesn't mean every single image has to be bread or beef related! Customers seek more than straight up product shots – they want to get a better understanding of who you are and how you think. Of course, it's great to show off your work, but potential customers will also want to see what you, your team and the business look like. This is especially important for businesses that service the public, such as gyms, restaurants, retailers, coffee shops, playgroups etc.

They also want to know what other clients say about you, as well as what sets you above the competition, so if you're an award-winning team, share the information!

People don't buy into a business for one reason only. Each one of us has our own set of 'purchase beacons' that trigger us to transact, so make sure to get the variety and balance of your images just right to communicate to as wide an audience as possible.

Be genuine

Online is the place to be the very best version of you. You have the time to take the perfect picture, edit it where necessary and even add a filter or effect. But ultimately, you have to be sincere. A discerning audience will see straight through posts that appear a bit desperate for likes.

If you have volunteered or raised money for charity and have received recognition for it, share it with your followers – but don't be a fake. Anything less than genuine and it can damage your brand. Avoid images or posts that might look 'staged' – your followers need to be able to trust you.

Get creative

It is sometimes hard to be inspired. When your working day is filled with meetings, finances, spreadsheets and so on, the idea of finding something exciting, engaging and creative to post can be daunting.

If you're feeling under par creativity-wise, check out the accounts of people who inspire you, particularly those that are established, popular and industry-related. You may see an image on another account that gives you that light bulb moment.

Consider alternative ways to photograph something, try different lighting angles and filters, but don't go overboard and ruin a perfectly good image with effects. Nor do you want to mislead followers with highly filtered images of your products. We all know the feeling of crushing disappointment when something we've seen and ordered online turns up and looks nothing like the photo and only fits the cat. Stay real. **See page 78 for inspiration on What to post.**

teethbylottie

❤ 💬 ✈

teethbylottie Many people drink hot water lemon in the morning as part of a diet, detoxification or to simply stimulate the digestive enzymes. While drinking lemon water in the morning is quite fashionable, did you know its causing irreversible damage to your teeth?

After a week of flu I too enjoyed many hot water lemon remedies, here's how to be savvy while doing so
x Don't consume daily, cut down
x Drink through a straw.
x Don't brush for 30 minutes after.
x Drink & swish with water after.
x Chew sugar free gum afterwards.
x Always use Fluoride toothpaste
x Use a fluoride rinse immediately after consumption.
#detox #health #womenshealth #diet #aciderosion #enamelerosion #erosion #totd #instadaily #rdh #dentaltherapist #healthysmile

Play the long game

Instagram allows a caption limit of up to 2,200 characters. My advice is to make the most of it and take advantage of this lengthier character count to write longer, more detailed and in-depth captions about your business. This isn't Twitter, so there's no need to abbreviate words to fit.

If you have a really important message or a call to action, try to do so in the first 125 characters where it will be immediately visible. Use the rest of your character allowance to go into further detail. These captions are your chance to educate and inspire potential customers.

However, do be wary of over writing captions. If your message for that particular post is short and sweet then leave it like that. There's no point posting waffle just to fill space, so judge it according to each post.

Planning your content

Planning your content is not only a great way to avoid last-minute panics, it also enables you to prepare the aesthetics and story for your imagery to ensure your feed always looks good and is varied and balanced.

There are plenty of free tools online to help you plan posts and schedule them to upload at a specific time. **www.later.com** even has a tool that allows you to play around with the grid, so you can work out the best aesthetic order for your images before posting.

Organising ahead isn't just helpful with imagery – it also gives you time to craft the perfect accompanying caption and choose the best hashtags while giving you the chance to check and double check your spelling.

☐ **Monday**
Lisa's anniversary

☐ **Tuesday**
Thank you gift from
Mr Smith

☐ **Wednesday**
Invisalign interview
with Susan

☐ **Thursday**
New photographs
of interior

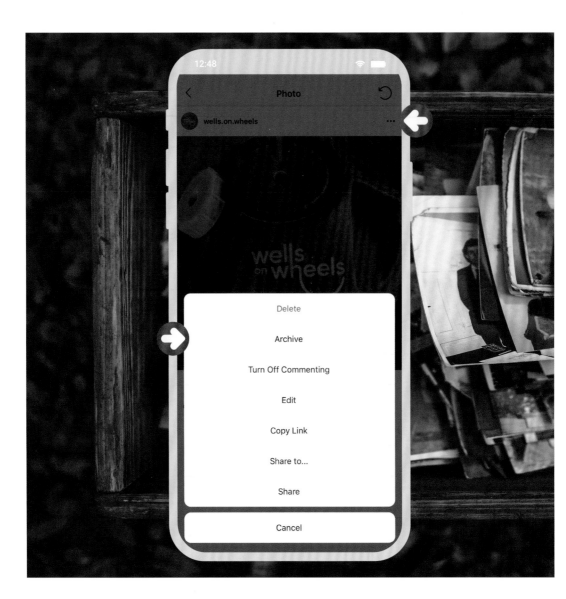

Archiving posts

As with all things new, you will never get it perfect the first time. Practice makes perfect and, as you continue on your Instagram journey, you will begin to see improvements in several ways – from the quality of your images, your captions and hashtags to how your interactions evolve with followers. The more you use Instagram, the more consistent you will become and your overall brand voice will be clearer.

As you embrace this newfound confidence, you may find yourself looking back on old posts in despair. Don't worry, you can archive a post and hide it.

To do this, open the image you want to archive on your feed, and click the three dots above the picture on the right-hand side. Click on **Archive**.

To unarchive a post, click on the clock icon on the top left. Select the post you want to unarchive and then click the three dots above the picture on the right-hand side and hit **Show on profile**.

When you archive a post it will still retain all of the likes and comments, which is why I suggest doing this rather than deleting a post permanently. Besides, archiving allows you to look back at old posts to see how far you've come and how much your Instagram skills have improved!

'But I don't want to be one of those annoying people....'

Self-promotion comes more easily to some than others and, for those of you less inclined to showcase your skills, Instagram can be somewhat daunting, particularly if you fear there is a risk of you becoming annoying.

We've all seen those accounts of people who post nothing but pictures of their dinner and desserts – yawn! I mean, unless it's a lovingly hand-reared avocado, grown on a magical mountaintop and watered with Gordon Ramsay's tears, no-one cares. The same goes for too many selfies. Whilst it's good to share pictures of yourself and your team when the occasion is right, selfie after selfie just screams narcissism and will make potential customers feel as though you care far more about yourself than them.

As long as your content is relevant, well thought out and not too self-obsessed, you'll be fine and not annoying.

IMAGERY

Inspire with imagery and storytelling

Instagram is a visual platform, a form of digital storytelling that creates a personal narrative to share with a target audience. Whilst you can always back up your post with explanatory text in your captions, ultimately it is the image that draws in the viewer, and many businesses have the opportunity to be very visual these days.

Think about how each image portrays you, your business and your brand. If you own a vegan restaurant, is this immediately clear to potential diners? Do your pictures tell followers what sort of dishes and meat-alternatives you offer? If your law firm specialises in family law, is that clear from the outset? The visual imagery should fully reflect who you are and the stories behind your pictures should inspire, motivating followers to enquire further and take action.

Taking great photos

You don't need to be a professional photographer to take great photos for Instagram, but there are a few easy tricks that will help you take the best shots you can.

- **Lighting.** Where possible, always use natural light instead of a flash. Your images will always look richer and brighter and are at less risk of looking washed out or unnatural.

- **Composition.** This refers to the arrangement of your photo and all the things within it, from the colours and textures to the shapes and other elements. Many photographers follow a simple composition principle called the 'Rule of Thirds'. This is an easy way to balance out your images using gridlines and intersections. Imagine your photo is broken down into a 3x3 grid as per the image to the left. By placing your image subject where the lines intersect, it balances out the image to enable the viewer to interact with it more naturally.

- **Viewpoint.** Most people tend to take photos straight on at eye level, which can sometimes make them feel flat and boring. If you want your photos to stand out, think about your angles. Try shooting your subject from above, or even crouch down and shoot upwards. Take your time and play around with photographing from different angles until you find a shot that works.

- **Framing.** Instagram crops your images square, so allow space around your subject to avoid cropping out something important. You may have to take a step back to allow for extra space. Remember you can always zoom in on Instagram if you have too much space, but you can't zoom out if you haven't allowed for the space in your shot.

Enhancing your photos

Now you've got the basics of photography nailed, there are a few more tricks of the trade you can utilise to make your images stand out.

- **Use a different camera.** Where possible, don't take your photos via Instagram. Your in-built phone camera is much better as most come with an HDR (High Dynamic Range) function that allows you to take photos with different pre-set exposures. You might not be able to do this with the Instagram camera. Alternatively, you can take your photos on any range of DSLR cameras and simply email them to yourself to upload.

- **Keep it steady.** Good clear photos need a firm hand. Consider investing in a mini tripod for your phone to get the perfect image. Many of them will have adaptable legs allowing you to attach it to tables, chairs or anything that is sturdy and most importantly still.

- **Online editing.** Whilst Instagram has basic in-app editing features, there are a number of free online editing tools to really help you create the perfect image. (**See page 250 on Recommended Apps**)

- **Add text.** Whether you have something inspirational you'd like to share or a general message for your followers, adding text can help your image stand out and is a good way of engaging users with imagery and text in one go. There are plenty of apps that can help you add text, such as **Instaquote**, **Over** and **Fontcandy**.

Using filters

Used properly, Instagram filters are a brilliant way to enhance your images. Not only can they enrich your photos but, used consistently, they can add cohesiveness to your whole grid, making you look professional and well put together. However, I don't usually recommend using filters on products, or on any of your before and after cases if you are in the aesthetics industry. Don't forget, it's never just about one photo, but your collection as a whole. Having a neon green image next to a moody monochrome one, amid some bright pink is not going to appear consistent.

Using filters is really easy. Once you've uploaded your image and cropped/resized it, click next and a list of different filters will appear along the bottom of your chosen picture. Tap on one to see how it affects the appearance of your image. You can change the intensity of the filter as well as brightness and contrast by clicking on edit. My personal favourite is the New York filter.

Be careful not to go overboard. If your image is unlit, adding a dark filter will reduce the quality of your post. Filters are meant to enhance and complement your picture, not change it completely.

Uploading multiple photos / videos in one post

Instagram allows you to post up to 10 photos or videos per post, which is great for sharing lots of photos at once for events or launches, for example, without filling your whole feed with the same type of picture. The first image looks just like a normal post, except for a row of dots at the bottom of the image showing how many pictures there are, which followers can then swipe through from left to right. Comments and likes will apply to the post as a whole rather than the individual pictures.

Uploading multiple pictures is easy. Simply go to your post photo icon as though uploading a normal post and click on **SELECT MULTIPLE**. Once clicked, you can upload up to 10 pictures or videos from your camera roll. They will appear with a little number indicating their order, but this can be changed later.

Once you've chosen your images, tap on **Next** to take you to the editing screen. You can apply the same filters to all the images or, if you click on each picture, you can edit them independently. You can then rearrange the photos into your preferred order by simply holding and dragging them to the left or right. If you want to delete any, just hold the image down and drag it to the bin icon.

When you're happy with your selection, click on next and write your caption and add your hashtags. (**See page 141 on Common business hashtags**). These will apply to the whole post. Finally, upload.

Case Studies   Product Range   Team Days Out

Location & Interiors   Tips   Funny Memes

Team   Awards   Selfies

Image organisation

A tidy desk is a tidy mind so the saying goes. In the rising world of digital, this remains the case - just replace the word desk for mobile phone or computer. Organisation is key to running your Instagram effectively and successfully and the first step is to ensure you use your folders properly.

Just like you would file paperwork, start filing your images into specific folders on your phone, for example 'Staff', 'Products', 'Events', etc. This allows you to start building a bank of content, which is quickly and easily accessible for you to repurpose whenever you need. Having a well-organised library of varied and usable images also allows you to post regularly, so you can keep engaging with your followers without having to scramble to find something to post. Simply refer to the folders on your phone. You can even create shared folders on some phones that allow team members to contribute and share their images into your folders. The most successful online influencers are extremely organised when it comes to this – so get filing!

Stock photography

Sometimes we simply don't have the time or inspiration to take the photos we want. In the rare event, this happens, and you feel truly stuck or uninspired, then you can turn to stock photography to fill the gap. It's not an ideal solution, as these photos are not exclusive to you. They may have been seen before on other websites or social media, and they can occasionally look staged - so do use sparingly.

I always recommend using your own, genuine photos for your feed and keep stock photography as a very last resort.

Free stock image sites:

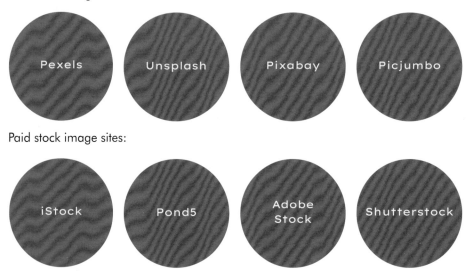

Paid stock image sites:

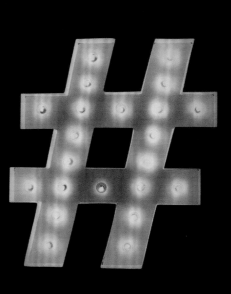

HASHTAGS

Embrace those hashtags

A hashtag is a word or phrase that is preceded by the hash mark # that helps to identify a keyword or topic of interest. Instagram then indexes all of these hashtags, allowing Instagram users to search and discover your account.

For example, let's say you love pugs – and who doesn't? If you type 'pugs' into the search bar on Instagram, you will see that for #pugs there are approximately 7,240,237 posts for you to search through.

In business terms, adding a hashtag to your posts means you will have a much greater chance of being found by people searching for that particular term, service or product. One study has found by adding just one hashtag to your post yields an average of 12.6% increase in engagement – which means more likes and comments for you!

Hashtags, as well as accounts, can now be followed, so adding hashtags such as #smallbiz, #shoplocal, #handmade can pull in any followers looking for those terms. **See page 141 on Common business hashtags**. #simples

#onlinebusiness

#homebusiness

#smallbusinesslove

#startupbusiness

#startupstory

On your new post, tap the  icon and paste your hashtags here

Hashtags in comments

Generally, Instagram users place their hashtags within their main caption and that's absolutely fine to do, especially if you're only using one or two tags. But if you're using a lot of hashtags in one post, it can appear messy and detract from the main message itself.

One trick is to put all of your hashtags in the first comment instead, leaving your image caption clean and clear. Another advantage of placing your hashtags in the comments is that they will soon get buried as more comments are made, but they will still be working away in the background, so you will still benefit even if they're not visible.

How many hashtags?

Instagram allows up to 30 hashtags on posts and 10 for stories. Whether you use all 30 every time is up for debate. Some marketeers think it can look spammy, especially if they are all in your main image caption. Others advise that businesses should take full advantage of this and post the full 30 on every single post.

The number of hashtags you use is entirely up to you but, for businesses looking to grow their brand, then more is definitely the way forward. A recent study has shown that using 11 or more hashtags increases engagement by an incredible 442%.

So, however many hashtags you decide to use, try to include at least 11 with every single post. If you're aiming for maximum engagement, hit that 30.

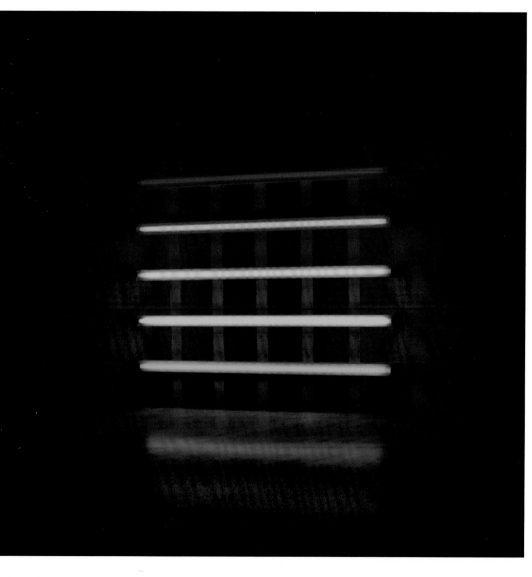

Common business hashtags

#onlinebusiness   #homebusiness   #smallbusinesslove   #startupbusiness

#startupstory   #businessowner   #smallbusinessowner   #beyourownboss

#entrepreneurial   #startups   #entrepreneursofinstagram   #entrepreneurspirit

#contentmarketing   #dreambigorgohome   #successmindset   #businesslife

#entrepreneurslife   #mycreativebiz   #creativeminds   #shopsmall   #satisfiedcustomer

#businessopportunity

On **page 67** I explained how you can search for hashtags. Search for hashtags that would be relevant to your posts and use them in your posts and Stories. To take your hashtag game up a notch, you can use a third party hashtag tool. Google '**Hashtag finder**' to find numerous free live hashtag databases.

'Flick' is a great paid service that helps you find, store and optimise Instagram hashtags using it's own algorithm. **www.flick.tech**

Hashtag bank

Make a list of hashtags you use regularly. It's a good idea to keep them all saved in one place for quick and easy access to save you the time and hassle of having to re-type them out each time you post.

Storing your most commonly used hashtags on your phone is the best place to start. The **Notes** App comes pre-installed on iPhones, and you can find similar apps to download for Android, such as **ColorNote** or **Evernote**. I personally use Evernote on an iPhone because it also syncs with the desktop apps on my computer and laptop.

Organise your different hashtags into groups such as 'Products' 'Events' 'Staff' etc and create a new note for each category where you can then input up to 30 hashtags. When you're ready to upload your next post, simply go into your notes and copy the ones you want to feed into your caption or comments and share!

Using email to store your hashtags is another great way of keeping everything easily accessible. As with Notes, simply create different emails for the different categories and send them to yourself. Create a folder within your email to store them for ease of access.

Your own hashtag

Some of the most successful online campaigns have been for brands that created their own hashtags, such as Coca Cola's #shareacoke, or Cancer Research UK's #nomakeupselfie. And you can create your own, too.

Think about a hashtag that could work for you or your business. Perhaps you already have a brand tagline or even a motto or saying that you are known for, or that is relevant to the brand. Check on both Twitter and Instagram that it has not already been taken for someone else's big campaign. It is unlikely you will find the perfect hashtag that has never been seen. There is always a chance that it has been used somewhere around the world but - so long as it's not overused because it's a generic hashtag, it should be ok.

Share your hashtag with a few trusted people you know before going public. They can help double-check that it makes sense as a hashtag and that the letters don't run together spelling out something it shouldn't. If only someone had told Susan Boyle's management team who were trying to promote her new album with #susanalbumparty…

Once you have decided on your hashtag, start sharing. Include it on all your Instagram posts and any other social media accounts you use. Remember that these hashtags can be used on print materials as well as online, such as flyers, posters, and banners. The aim is to get the hashtag associated with your brand and get people accustomed to seeing it so that, when they post something about you or your business, they'll automatically think to include your hashtag.

Remember to regularly search the hashtag on Instagram, so you can respond and reply to anyone appropriate, as there are lots of people who may have used a hashtag that doesn't apply to them. For example, #wellsonwheels is used by many other types of businesses and we only respond to photos that are relevant to the charity by either liking the images or commenting and resharing.

STAY CONNECTED

Replying and making comments

One of the most appealing aspects of Instagram is its ability to facilitate an immediate connection and engagement with your audience. So, do take time to interact with them. Regularly check your notifications for comments. Instagram will let you know when you have a comment by way of a little speech-bubble above the heart icon on your account. It may be an enquiry about a specific product or simply a happy client saying 'thank you'. Either way, replying to followers and responding to comments sends out a positive message to everyone browsing your account. It shows that you're responsive, approachable and that you care about your customers. If you treat them this well on social media, chances are you are an empathetic team in real-life, too!

A little trick you can try: Instead of replying right away, hold off until you make your next post. Once you have made your next post, go back to the previous post and reply to each person who commented. When they receive a notification that you replied to a comment, their natural reaction may be to click on your profile again. When they do, they will see your new post and possibly engage with it again.

Deleting spammy or unwelcome comments

Email spam is almost as old as email itself and unwanted comments can be a pain on Instagram, too. As your brand and Instagram account grows, you will find that lots of people will want to piggyback on your success. They'll often do this by hijacking a popular post and commenting purely for their own agenda. Sometimes, there will be a legitimate face behind the comment, trying everything they can to get noticed. Other times, the comments will come from automated spam bots targeting high engagement posts. Whilst the Instagram algorithm is constantly evolving to deal with spam, it is unlikely to disappear any time soon. If you notice a comment like this on one of your posts, simply delete and move on. The same applies to unwelcome comments.

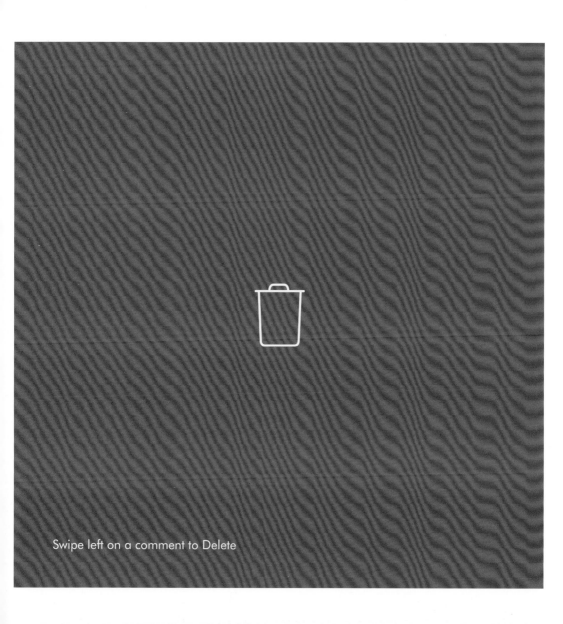

Swipe left on a comment to Delete

Check your inbox for DMs

Direct messages (DMs) can be easily missed on Instagram, so make sure to check in frequently, as there may be a potential customer waiting to hear back. To check your messages, simply click on the paper aeroplane icon on the top right corner of your feed. Responding in a timely and friendly manner with all the necessary information instils confidence in people. If it takes you a week to reply, potential customers may wonder about the sort of service you will offer in the future. If you can't reply to a message quickly, you give the impression that their business is not important to you. Leave it too long and they may have already started looking elsewhere.

Make sure you or someone in your team is tasked with replying to DMs as you would with emails. Replies should be sent as soon as possible. Studies suggest that 78% of customers buy from the first responder.

On your  view, click on ▽ to read DMs

Perfect scripted responses

At the beginning of any social media journey, it can be very exciting when you start getting likes and comments on your posts and messages in your inbox. Knowing that any one of these could be a potential lead might mean we respond with full passion and detail to every single enquiry.

However, over time 'reply fatigue' can kick in as you find yourself dealing with so-called 'price checkers'. The initial buzz of engaging with potential customers can begin to wear off. This will show as responses get weaker and comments take longer to reply to, if at all. Nobody ever really knows which of these leads could turn into a client or an endorsement, so it is important to remember how a lazy reply can affect your brand in the long term. We can all remember at least one time we weren't given the right attention when we had the full intention of buying, so make sure you treat every enquiry with the attentiveness that you yourself would wish to receive.

To combat this reply fatigue, start crafting some pre-written responses for the most common questions and have them ready to send. You could even use these replies for email responses at reception in the business or vice versa if you already have canned email responses. Take your time to perfect them and ensure you have the answers to frequently asked questions, including expected outcome, price range, what to do next and everything in between. Your responses should flow well and have a consistent tone of voice throughout and, most importantly, spell check everything! Save these responses in your phone notes so that you can copy and paste them to potential enquiries when needed or, even better, use **Quick replies.**

Turn over to learn more about Quick replies.

Quick replies

Quick replies are pre-written responses (also known as canned responses) that can save you a lot of time when replying to commonly asked questions.

To create a quick reply, tap on the + icon to reveal the Quick reply icon in the message field of the chat/DM screen. **See page 152 on Direct messages**. The first time you set up a quick reply, you will usually see a screen that briefly explains the Quick replies feature. Tap New quick reply or the + icon to set up your first reply.

After you have created at least one quick reply, you'll see a list of all of the replies you have saved. To add a new one, tap the + button on the pop-up screen.

To create your quick reply, type the pre-scripted message you want to use in the Message field. Then give this shortcut a name in the shortcut field. The shortcut shouldn't exceed 15 characters in length. Then tap on **Save**. Every time you type the shortcut name in a Direct Message e.g. deluxe dog grooming, price, the option to paste in the pre-scripted message will appear.

Click ⌁ to open your DM window

Open a message and tap ⊕ then ⬚ to open Quick replies

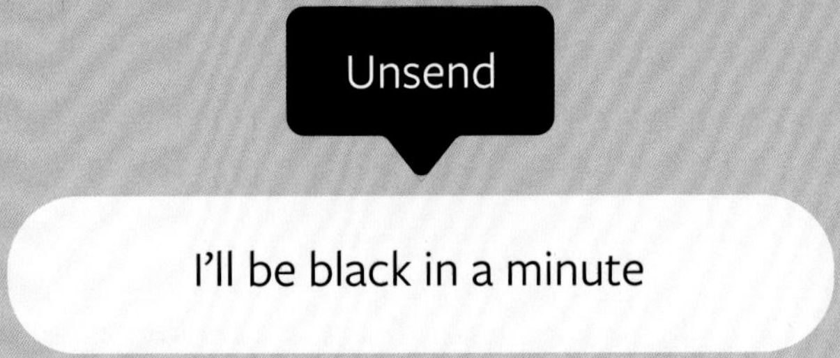

Hold down on your message to reveal the Unsend option

Unsending a message

We've all been there, pressed **send** before we meant to or sent something to the wrong person. Luckily, Instagram has devised a tool that allows you to 'unsend' a message. Mind you, this only works if the recipient hasn't already seen it – you can unsend, but they can't 'un-see'.

To unsend a message, simply tap and hold on the message and select **Unsend**. This means the message will no longer be visible to anyone included in that conversation, and you just have to hope that you acted quickly enough before anyone had a chance to see it.

Get tagging

'Tagging' is pretty much what it says on the tin - an option on Instagram that allows you to 'tag' another Instagram user. It draws their attention to your post as well as letting other followers see who you've tagged.

Tagging is a great tool to engage with your followers and a wider audience. You can tag anyone you like, but make sure to keep it relevant – you can tag colleagues, customers and even other brands you work with. Make sure to only tag customers if you are re-sharing their own post about you, or if you have their explicit consent to do so.

First, you need to know how to tag, which is actually very simple – when you're uploading your image or video, just beneath where you type your caption there is an option to **Tag people**. Click on this and it will take you to a new screen where you can tap anywhere on the picture to place your tag; this can be a person, product or a specific area of your picture. Once you've chosen your area, a search bar will appear with a little tag that says **Search for a person**. Just start typing in the name of the account you want to tag, choose from the dropdown list that appears and voila, you have tagged someone!

You can tag anyone you want, just don't overdo it and ensure the tags are representative of what you are posting. Remember, just as you can tag people, they can tag you so make an effort to reply to anyone who tags you. This makes for great engagement, and a happy customer or a positive testimonial means free promotion for you and your brand.

Go ahead and tag me in photos and videos of your copy of this book:
@shaz.memon

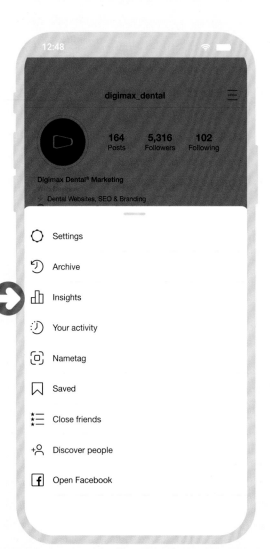

digimax_dental

164 Posts **5,316** Followers **102** Following

Digimax Dental® Marketing

Dental Websites, SEO & Branding

○ Settings

⟳ Archive

⬚ Insights

⟳ Your activity

⬚ Nametag

🔖 Saved

≔ Close friends

+♂ Discover people

f Open Facebook

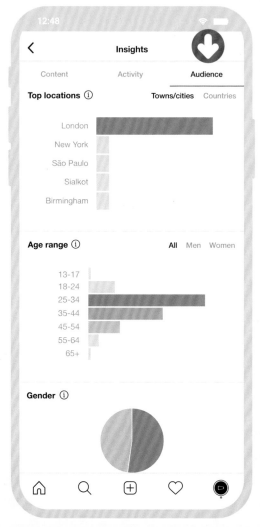

12:48

Insights

Content   Activity   **Audience**

Top locations ⓘ   Towns/cities   Countries

London
New York
São Paulo
Sialkot
Birmingham

Age range ⓘ   All   Men   Women

13-17
18-24
25-34
35-44
45-54
55-64
65+

Gender ⓘ

Analysing your audience

Understanding your audience will help you to choose more relevant content to post, which will in turn boost engagement and follower numbers. Instagram Analytics is an inbuilt tool that goes beyond simply telling you which of your posts has the most likes or comments. It looks into your audience's demographics and their behaviours and patterns. By taking a much broader look at your account, it allows you to analyse the data so that you can make well-informed decisions and make adjustments where necessary to the type of content you post.

To access Insights from your profile page, click on the menu at the top right and choose the little graph icon labelled **Insights**. Here you will find data on your followers including **Top Locations** for both cities and countries, **Age range** and **Gender** as well as the times when your **Followers** are most active.

If you want to find data for a single post, go to that post in your feed and tap on **View Insights** beneath it on the left.

Analysing your audience continued

Using Instagram Insights is a fantastic way to tailor your content and develop a marketing strategy. Having insight into your overall audience, based on their gender, age range, location and online usage times, can help you better understand your followers. You can then, in turn, assess whether you're reaching your preferred target audience.

Look out for patterns showing what time of day your followers are most online and post content during these periods to maximise reach and engagement. You can even use this data to plan ahead and schedule your posts to upload during these key times. **See page 110 on Planning your content**.

Look at the data for your post engagements to see what content works well. You might find that posts with people perform far better than posts without. You can look at the number of likes and comments, impressions and reach and ratio of engagement to reach to help you work out which of your posts perform the best.

Instagram engagement pods

An Instagram Pod is essentially a direct message between a group of 15-20 people, similar to a WhatsApp group, but for Instagram. Different Pods' rules can vary, but generally, whenever a user posts something new, that post is shared in the direct message and everyone within the group is required to like or comment on it. This is mutually beneficial for everyone in the group as it goes both ways for everyone involved. Being part of a group guaranteed to like your posts helps your posts to appear more popular and even rise to the top of your followers' feeds.

Think of it like texting a friend to say: 'My post only has six likes, can you please comment?' You're asking them to help with engagement and you do the same for them in return – except with Pods you might have to like up to 20 or 30 posts a day.

There are a few things to consider when starting a Pod. The first is to find users who have a similar following count to yourself, so start by looking at people you know who fall into this category and who would be interested in joining your Pod. You can also find potential 'Pod-ees' by searching for people who use similar hashtags to you. Chances are you're both aiming to appeal to a similar demographic. Once you've got a list of people you'd like to approach, send a DM with a view to striking up a relationship. When you have enough people on board, you can start your Pod.

I am not encouraging the use of Pods, because it is time consuming and a little 'manufactured'. That said, I know many users who love using pods for the speed in which 'likes' can be collected.

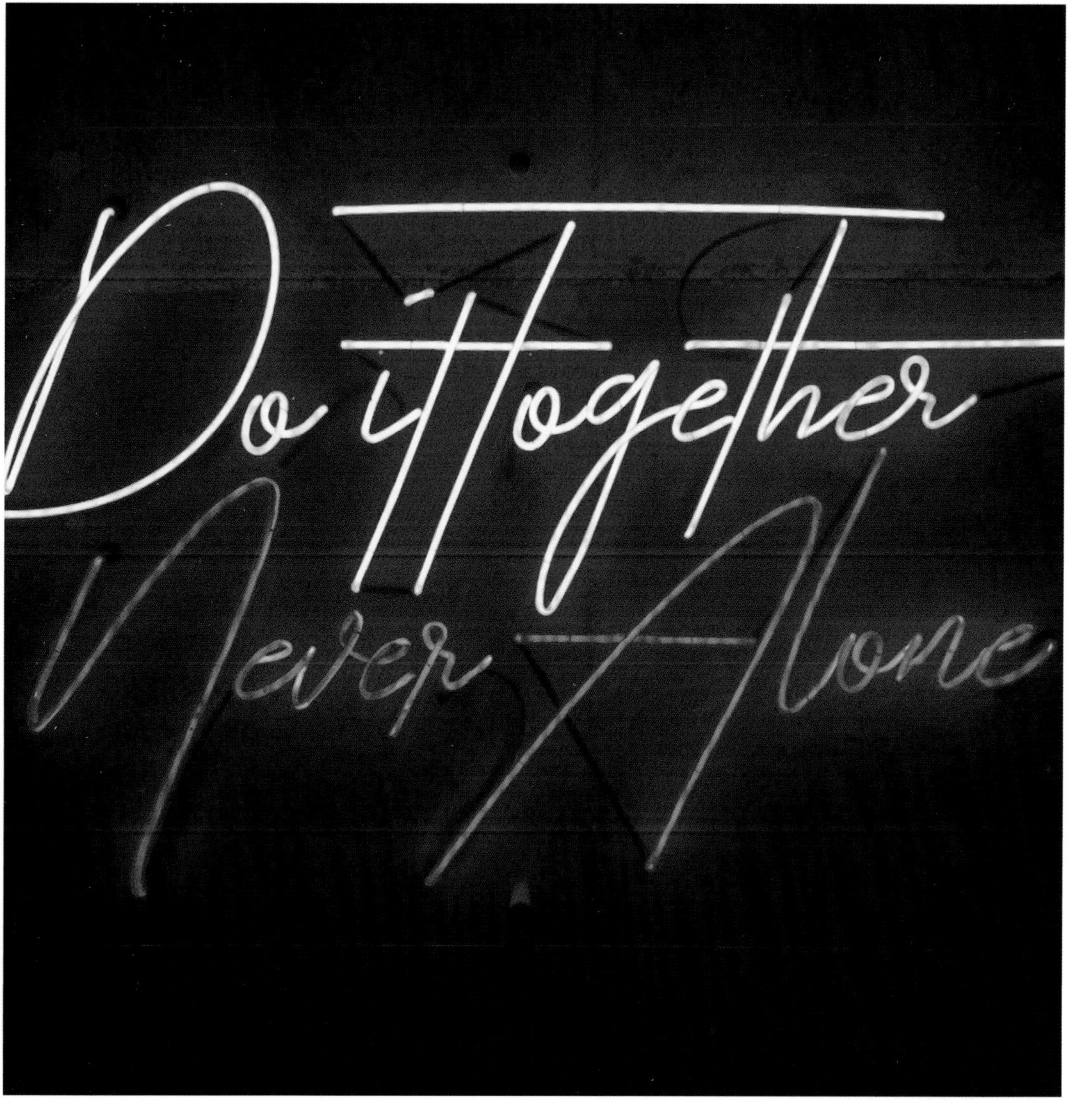
Do it Together
Never Alone

BUILD YOUR BRAND

Personal branding

If you are looking to build your personal brand on Instagram, you will need a brand identity to make it easier for your followers and clients to recognise you. This includes having a professional, well-designed logo. You may have seen lots of logos on Instagram for competitor businesses, ranging from the homemade to the professional.

A brand identity package from a logo designer should include your logo files in a number of digital file formats – PNG, JPG, EPS, AI, and PDF. The files you receive should be a mix of high resolution (for high definition printing) as well as web quality for use online. You should also receive social media versions for use on any social media accounts, including a version that works well in a circle profile photo on Instagram.

I would advocate investing in the creation of a professional brand identity.

Add your location

Whenever you upload a post, it's a good idea to add your locations as it helps potential customers find you. This is especially true if you have multiple business locations. According to statistics, posts with a tagged location result in 79% higher engagement than those without a tagged location.

Adding your location is really simple. Simply go to your post photo icon as though uploading a normal post, after clicking **Next**, click on **Add location**. Search your location and tap to add it to your post!

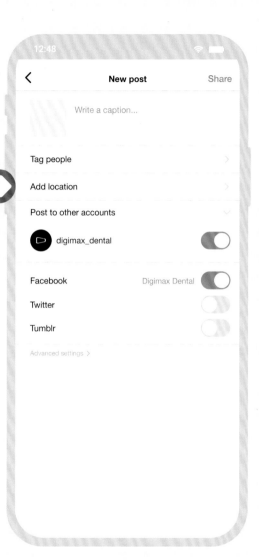

Using an influencer

At some point during your social media journey, you will no doubt have come across the term 'influencer'. An influencer is often someone with a large following, who has the power to 'influence' purchase decisions by way of authority, knowledge, and relationship with their audience. In terms of Instagram, this is largely reflected by their number of followers – the more followers an influencer has, the larger the potential market to which a brand or service can promote. But it isn't always about numbers. The quality of their followers is just as important as reach – who are they appealing to? If their base following is made up of teenagers, you're unlikely to get a lot of business that way.

Good influencer marketing should always be transparent about paid content and both sides need to be clear on the relationship from the start. Sadly, some influencers have been known to make promises of promotion in exchange for free or discounted products and services without actually following through. To avoid this, aim to build a real relationship with them and ensure they understand clearly you are exchanging 'currency' for the work and that it is important for you that they deliver on their promises of promoting you in return.

If you are offering to pay with a high-value exchange or even hard cash, it's always a good idea to draw up a basic contract – one page can suffice, outlining the deal to ensure that both sides are on the same page. And finally, please ensure that how you are using an influencer meets regulatory expectations. The Advertising Standards Authority (ASA) publishes a guide to help everyone understand the boundaries. The Influencers Guide adds clarity to this form of marketing and outlines what the rules demand.

Advertising Standards Authority (ASA) on working with influencers

The ASA has published a guide to help everyone understand the boundaries. The Influencer's Guide adds clarity to this form of marketing, making clear what the rules demand. Developed in collaboration with the Competition and Markets Authority (CMA), it was published in reaction to the exponential growth of influencer marketing.

The guidance outlines the rules, what it is the ASA considers is an advert as well as offers suggestions as to how brands can make clear that ads are ads.

Chief executive of the ASA, Guy Parker, explains: 'People shouldn't have to play the detective to work out if they're being advertised to. That means the status of a tweet, blog, vlog, Instagram post or Story should be clear.'

In essence, honesty is the best policy and openness a necessity. Paid partnerships need to be made clear.

Making paid partnerships clear

Instagram has launched a **Branded content** feature to help users identify when an influencer on Instagram has been paid to endorse a product or service.

Instagram writes: 'We define branded content as a creator or publisher's content that features or is influenced by a business partner for an exchange of value (for example, where the business partner has paid the creator or publisher).

'Our policies require creators and publishers to tag business partners in their branded content posts when there's an exchange of value between a creator or publisher and a business partner.'

If someone influential is receiving services or products for free or highly discounted services by your business, they should tag you as a 'Business Partner' so this partnership is publicly declared on their post. Tagged posts have a clear label – 'Paid partnership with'

For the influencer to do this, on the screen where they write a caption on the post, tap **Advanced Settings > Tag Business Partner** as well as switching on **Allow business partner to promote.** Switching this on means you can run a paid promotion to show off the endorsement to a wider audience. **Turn over for more information on Paid promotions.**

Instagram

---

 digimax_dental
Paid partnership with **Singingdentist** ✔

...

309 Likes

digimax_dental This is an example of how a paid
partnership appears when publicly declared.

6 MINUTES AGO ·

Paid post promotions get more visibility

Considering that Instagram users engage 10 times more with brands than they do on Facebook, it is the perfect platform to test out paid advertising. Sponsoring an advert on Instagram is also known as a promoted post, which can be a high-performing post of yours that you would like to share with a wider audience. Or, it can be a targeted post created for a specific reason, such as a new service or special offer.

If you have a post that is advertising an event such as a product launch, consider allocating some of your marketing budget to boosting that post so that it can reach a much wider audience.

To boost a post, head to your profile page and click **Promotions**. Tap **Create Promotion** at the bottom. Choose the post you'd like to promote and then tap **Next**.

Fill in the details of your promotion by setting the **Destination** (where your audience will be directed when they see your post e.g Profile / Website or Direct messages), **Audience** (who you want to target), **Budget** (how much you would like to spend) and **Duration** (how long you wish your promotion to run). Tap **Next** once you've completed these details.

To complete your promotion, tap **Create Promotion**.

Your advert won't go live immediately. It will be submitted for review to ensure it meets Instagram's ad policy. Once approved, your promotion will go live.

Promotions

Click on **Promotions** to get started

Paid Story promotions

To boost an active Story, tap your profile picture in the top left to open then at the bottom of the screen tap on **More > Promote**.

Fill in the details of your promotion by setting the **Destination** (where your audience will be directed when they see your post e.g. Profile/Website or Direct messages), **Audience** (who you want to target), **Budget** (how much you would like to spend) and **Duration** (how long you wish your promotion to run). Tap **Next** once you've completed these details.

To complete your promotion, tap **Create Promotion**.

Promoted Stories will run as long for as you wish – simply set the Duration time – whereas the active Story on your profile will expire after 24 hours as usual.

Selling products on Instagram

It is now possible to sell products on Instagram directly from your posts. You can offer users a seamless buying experience through the checkout feature. Instagram shoppable posts are marked with a 'Tap to View Products' pop-up or small white circle with a shopping bag icon enabling users to browse your 'Shop' feed directly from your Instagram profile.

Before you can get selling you'll need to be approved for Instagram shopping to feature your products in posts and stories. In order to be approved you'll need to fulfil certain requirements such agreeing to Instagram's commerce policies and having a connected Facebook account (**See page 59 on connecting your Facebook Account**)

This feature is rapidly evolving so for the most up-to-date, step-by-step instructions go to Instagrams Help Centre and search 'Set Up Requirements for Shopping on Instagram' for full details, or search YouTube for help in setting up a store of your own. Happy Selling!

Attracting high value clients

Many business owners will have a clear idea of their target market and your goal with Instagram may be to attract more high-value clients, especially if you are selling to, or servicing the luxury market.

The way to do this is to appeal to such clients. Remember the Power of 9 on page 79 - if a potentially high-value client visits your page, do those first 9 images show the quality of product or level of service with which they would want to engage? Have you included positive testimonials from previous clients you have satisfied? Does your account show images of a lifestyle your chosen clients are accustomed to?

For example, if you are in the high-end hospitality industry, have you shown the 5 star nature of your offering – the size of the suites, the quality of the soft furnishings, the genuine smiles of the staff and high levels of customer service? Is there a spa on-site? What brands do the therapists use? Any potential client will want to feel assured that you are offering them the type of very high-end service that they will be expecting.

Once you have built your followers and have a strong account, you can look at paid advertising for your brand. Remember to make any adverts or promotions look high-end to match the services you are offering. Like attracts like and cheap, gimmicky adverts are unlikely to bring you the kind of client you're looking for.

Customers have influence

The average number of followers for a personal Instagram account is 150 – ordinarily made up of friends and family. This doesn't make them any less important or less influential. In fact, they have a greater influence for you because the people they are connected with on social media are more likely to take notice of their posts and engage with them. If your customers are on Instagram, giving them easy ways to post about your products and services is a great way to influence these friends and family with their own posts.

If you are a hairstylist, for example, you could take a video with your client showing off their new hairstyle. Ask them how happy they are with their new style – post it on your Story (**See page 214 on Instagram stories**) and tag them. Chances are they're delighted with their new look and will be keen to re-share it with everyone they know. Remember to always get their consent first before filming and posting it on your account.

If your business is more product related, think of ways to make customers want to take photos of your product and share with their friends, for example, if you are a restaurant you can have fun with your dishes to make it easy your for customers to tag you #supersizedsundaesundays or #tastytacotuesdaytreats anyone!?

Happy customers are your best form of advertising and this first-hand promotion on Instagram is a huge growth method for any business to gain more followers.

Can Instagram be outsourced?

There are many agencies and freelancers willing to take Instagram management off your hands and oversee your account. But that doesn't mean you should. Quite simply, Instagram is about being real and genuine with your followers. It's the opportunity to engage directly with potential customers and, unless you're outsourcing to an ex-industry professional, the chances are they're never going to do as good a job as you or your team.

Also, many of your posts will be based around your business persona, your services, and the products, so unless you have someone following you around with a camera, you'll still need to take the time to collate the imagery you want to upload and send it to the agency. Not only that, but it's also likely you'll need to explain the different business terms and jargon. They might not be able to answer a direct enquiry, as they won't have the necessary information, so this will ultimately come back to you anyway. Save yourself the time and added hassle of managing someone else managing your account and just do it yourself. Besides, by the time you get to the end of this book, you'll know pretty much everything you need to know anyway!

What kind of results can you expect?

Instagram takes time to develop and there is no overnight success story. Done properly, however, it allows you to build real relationships with your followers, which may lead you to finding more of the type of customers or clients you'd like.

You will start receiving enquiries as your follower numbers grow and, ultimately, you'll get out of it what you put in.

I have worked with certain industry professionals who generate 80% of their new business on Instagram alone, but I also know others that tend to attract only one or two new clients a month – so your results will be largely dictated not only by your industry and profession, but also by your effort. Also, bear in mind how large your actual target market is, the demand for your services and products and your location. If you are a health food store situated in a more rural location you are unlikely to see the same sort of results as a city-based retailer.

I have more than one location

If you have more than one location for your business, but they are part of the same brand name, then one centrally managed Instagram account is fine. It is easier to grow one account than multiple individual accounts for each location. With this, comes a little more responsibility. You need to ensure posts cater for the brand as a whole and not cause confusion for your customers.

If, for example, you offer film and photography services at one location, but only photography at the other you need to be clear in the visible small print which location this relates to. You also need to make it easy to see all the locations. The bio is the best place for this and the next best place is in your posts – the first 9 squares should always make it obvious that you have multiple locations. **See page 79 on the Power of 9**.

If you have multiple locations with varied names and different websites, then you need to treat these businesses separately and give them their own individual Instagram accounts.

FILMING

Why use video?

After the resounding success of Instagram as a photo-sharing site, it was inevitable that video would soon follow. In 2013, Instagram allowed users to upload 15-second video clips, which has now increased to a full minute.

First and foremost, video allows you to share much more in-depth stories with a complexity that a single image is unable to convey. It gives you the ability to tell an engaging story via multiple images, music, and even interviews and customer testimonials.

Video works especially well for brands looking to showcase their products and services, drive engagement and interact in a way your competitors might not yet be utilising.

Video usage statistics

Check out some of these incredible statistics that confirm video marketing is the future.

95%
of a message is retained compared to only 10% when reading text

72%
would rather learn about a service by way of video

48%
more views on social media posts which contain video

1200%
more sharing of videos compared to text and images

85%
of consumers want to see more video content from brands

97%
of marketers say video works better at converting audiences

64%
of consumers will make a purchase after watching a video on social media

1.5x
of users are more likely to watch video on their mobile phones

83%
of marketers say video gives them a good ROI

Film like a pro

Creating great videos for Instagram is very similar to taking great photos – you need to focus on good lighting, composition and an interesting subject matter. The only difference is, you'll need up to 60 seconds of footage rather than a single image. Ensure you plan to make your filming experience run smoothly and enjoyably.

- **Storyboard your video**. Start by planning out what you want your video to contain. You can write this out in a list or storyboard it with little sketches. This allows you to see if the order works well and if there's anything you've missed out.

- **Filming people**. If you're interviewing someone, write your list of questions in advance and give them a chance to consider their responses before pressing record, but don't let them pre-plan the full answer. Unless your interviewee is a trained actor, trying to 'learn' their lines before filming always comes across as stilted and disingenuous. You want them to come across as naturally as possible.

- **Capturing B-roll**. 'B-roll' is a term that professional filmmakers use for their secondary footage. For example, if an interviewee is the focus of your video, and they start to talk about how your business delivered a highly tailored service, insert footage of maybe a team member smiling and enthusiastically serving a client. Think about what other imagery you might need to accompany their interview – anything that helps keep the video interesting and engaging will work.

- **Soundcheck**. If you're planning on using audio in your video – music or someone talking – make sure the quality is crisp and clear. For music, use the best quality track you can, and make sure you familiarise yourself with music licensing rights first. If you're interviewing someone, do a couple of test takes and play it back to hear how it sounds. We often tend to block out general office noise, such as the hum of an air conditioner unit or the traffic outside, but played back on video, every clink, clank, and clunk can be noticeable, so try to find the quietest room possible.

More video tips

Once you've got to grips with the basics of filming, there are a few more tips to help make your videos stand out and maximise engagement potential.

- **Make the first seconds count**. Most Instagram users scroll through their feed quite quickly, so don't open with slow or boring shots. Choose something that captures attention.

- **Add text**. Instagram mutes videos by default, meaning that if you want to hear what's being said you have to manually tap the post to allow sound. For people who are sneaking a look at their feed while they're at work, this minimises their chances of being caught by the boss! But it also means they might skip past your video, so adding text or subtitles to complement the imagery is a great way of holding their attention for longer.

- **Tell your story**. What are you hoping to achieve with your video? Are you trying to get more followers? Are you promoting a new product? Are you moving office? Having a clear idea of what you want as the outcome will have an enormous bearing on the sort of content to include and the structure of your video.

- **Be consistent**. If you have a certain look or style across your images, try to incorporate this into your videos whatever you use to represent your brand on a daily basis. This may be a specific font or a colour. Keep it consistent across all media.

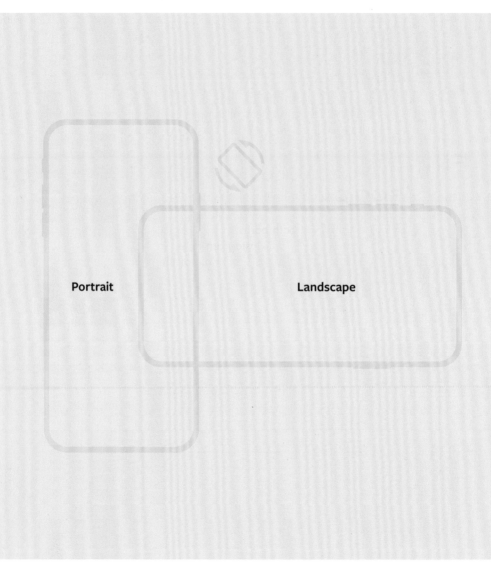

Portrait

Landscape

Filming portrait or landscape?

Instagram allows you to upload both portrait and landscape videos, so which should you use? If the video is for your main Instagram feed, then I recommend filming in landscape, focusing the core content in the middle of the frame, which allows more space to crop square.

I highly encourage using Instagram Stories and IGTV. For this, film in portrait. Cropping to portrait can affect the video negatively (unless you originally filmed it in portrait view) but, if done carefully, you can minimise any issues for a portrait video, such as centralising the subject as much as possible.

If you are filming your videos from your smartphone, then it is simple to film in portrait. But if you are hiring a professional videographer, they will most certainly choose to film in landscape, so do let them know how and where you intend to use the final films.

Editing clips

Whilst it's perfectly fine to simply film one long take (up to 60 seconds) the best videos are the ones that have been edited together using multiple clips to tell the story. There are plenty of editing apps to help you with this (**See page 250 on Recommended apps**) alternatively you can use the in-feed Instagram app to edit it all so instead of doing your filming via your phone camera and editing in a separate app, you can do it all with Instagram itself.

To get started simply tap the + sign at the bottom of your the app and choose **Video**. Then simply press and hold to record your clip and release when you're finished. You can record as many clips as you like (up to 60 seconds total) and Instagram will merge them all for you in the order you recorded them.

Once you're happy with the final result, you can choose whether or not to stabilise the footage, choose your sound options and add your filters. All that's left to do then is add your caption, hashtags, and locations and then publish!

If you do choose to edit on a separate app, there are a few technical things to remember for your video. Make sure you use the correct dimensions. Most phone cameras film at 1920x1080 pixels which is a 16:9 aspect ratio. There are three size options for Instagram

1. Square video: 600px x 600px – 1:1 aspect ratio

2. Horizontal video: 600px x 315px – 1.9:1 aspect ratio

3. Vertical video: 600px x 750px – 4:5 aspect ratio

When you export your video choose either a .mp4 or .mov format, keep the video size under 4GB and a maximum frame rate of 30fps.

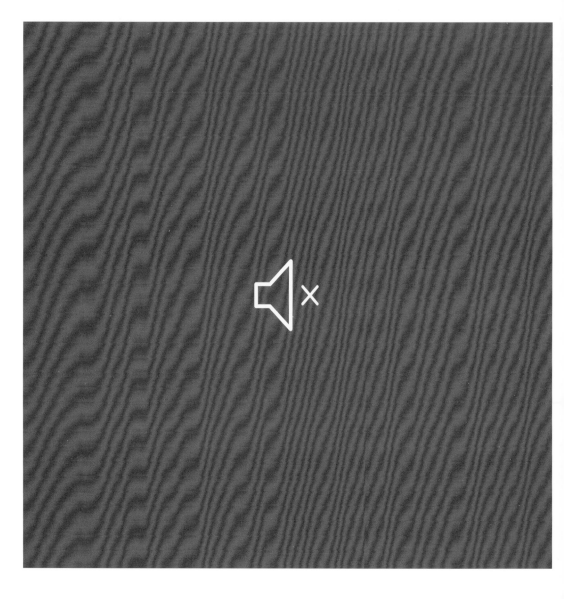

Editing your video with sound off

Planning your video without sound before shooting will help the process go more smoothly, as it allows you to ask the question of whether each shot speaks for itself without further explanation. If you feel like the odd word or sentence here or there would help, you can add text during the editing process or even drop in a sticker or two. **See page 236 on Polls, questions, love rating, quizzes and more!**

You can remove the audio on any video you upload to Instagram from within the platform itself by simply tapping on the speaker icon at the top of your screen. You can turn the sound back on by tapping the speaker again. I have found this useful when I have captured a video for its visual value, but the sound in the background of people talking might be distracting. You can mute the sound, and even add music in its place. **See page 232 on Adding Music.**

Recording your day

If you want to give your followers a behind-the-scenes look at your business, it doesn't all have to be done at once. You can record different clips throughout the day and edit them together at the end. Think about the aspects of your brand you want them to see or know about.

You could even create a recurring theme like 'Behind the Scenes' – just consider it like your very own TV show! **See page 235 on IGTV.**

Anything that shows you doing what you do best makes for great viewing. Your followers will love feeling like they're getting an exclusive peek at something and the more genuine and engaging you are, the more likely they are to want to work with you or buy from you.

INSTAGRAM STORIES

Instagram Stories

Instagram Stories is a feature that allows users to post photos and videos in a slideshow format that disappears after 24 hours. This is a great feature that lets you share highlights of your day or special moments quickly and easily, that you might not want to keep permanently on your feed. Also, giving users a little 'sneak peek' into your day and what's happening behind the scenes gives a sense of exclusivity, making them feel special to be privy to these aspects of your life or brand.

There are numerous benefits to posting Stories. The first is that there are more than 200 million active users on stories daily. Even better is that they are discoverable, which means that people who don't follow you can still see them. This is a great way to reach out to new potential customers who, if they enjoy your Story, may be more inclined to follow your account. As with standard posts, you can even add hashtags, so make sure you use something relevant that will appeal to the type of people you are hoping to attract.

A report by TechCrunch showed that one in five Instagram Stories shared by a brand received a direct reply, which shows that Stories is an incredible tool for direct engagement with your audience.

For accounts with more than 10,000 followers, you can even include a 'Swipe up' link to your website. If you have fewer than this, don't worry, when the feature was first rolled out it was only available to accounts with more than one million followers, so chances are this number could drop one day.

Another great thing about Instagram Stories are all the cool little filters, stickers and tools it comes with – and there are new features being added regularly! Here are the popular ones:

- **Superzoom.** This is a fun and quirky feature that allows you to record a three-second video of you quickly zooming in on an object or person with a dramatic sound effect. Try superzooming on your face for a comedy reaction.

- **Boomerang.** This is a very enjoyable feature that takes really short, super-fast bursts of photos and then stitches them together into a mini video that plays forwards and then backward repeatedly.

- **Rewind.** This is a brilliant tool that allows you to play your videos in reverse allowing you to have a lot of fun and get really creative. Imagine belly flopping out of a pool, or un-cooking your dinner.

- **Interactive poll stickers.** You can now add interactive poll stickers to your IG stories so that your followers can vote and see real-time results on any questions you ask. **See page 236 on Polls, questions, love rating, quizzes and more!**

Stories needn't be a Spielberg

Instagram Stories stay live for 24 hours. They don't need to be perfectly edited.

It's comforting to know that people tend to race through Stories so you know that this audience is entirely forgiving of a 'rough cut' kind of post.

This makes it easier for you to not hold back in posting video content that doesn't look like a high-quality production. Instagram Stories are absolutely fine to appear as if they were made 'on the fly'.

I prefer to keep high-quality videos in my main feed or on our IGTV channel (**See page 235 on IGTV**) and I use Stories for quick videos where I haven't necessarily spent a long time planning the composition.

To start a Story click your profile picture in the top left

Starting a Story

Creating an Instagram Story is not only easy – it can be fun too!

To get started, click on your profile picture on the top left of your screen, with the small blue '+' icon on it. Once the Story camera is open take your photo or record your video just like you would a normal post and you can add filters, text and even drawings to the post. (**See page 236 on Polls, questions, love rating, quizzes and more!**)

When you're ready to share, simply tap **Your Story** on the bottom left of your screen.

Instead, if you would like to broadcast your Story **LIVE,** click the **LIVE** text at the bottom of the screen. Before you go live, make sure to plan what you will say or showcase. It's a good idea to promote your live event ahead of time to get people tuning in. Ensure that your phone is steady, maybe even set up on a tripod with no obstructions in the way of the camera lens. You can go live for questions and answers, or even cover a launch day to show people what they are missing out on.

Repost a Story

Reposting Instagram Stories is a quick and simple way to fill your own Stories with beautiful imagery and footage created by other people, but it only works if they have tagged or mentioned you in their post.

When you're mentioned in someone else's Story, you'll receive a notification in your direct message inbox. Within the message will be an option to **Add This to Your Story**, Tap on this and the post will become a sticker with a customisable background within your Stories editor. Now you can add a bit of your own flair by tap and dragging into a new position, pinching the screen to resize it, adding stickers, GIFS, text, hashtags, and mentions.

When you're ready to share, simply tap **Your Story** on the bottom left of your screen.

Add This to Your Story >

Tap **Add This to Your Story** to reshare a Story you have been mentioned in

@MENTION

In Stories, tap 🙂 followed by

How to mention someone

Just as with sharing photos, you can add captions and mentions to your videos. Essentially the same as tagging, (**See page 160 on Tagging**) when you mention someone in your Story (**See page 214 on Instagram Stories**) their username will appear in your Story with a line underneath. This allows anyone who sees your Story to tap their name to go straight to their profile. The person you've mentioned will get a notification that you've done so, and they will receive a direct message from you that includes a preview of the Story.

You can mention up to 10 people and they'll all be notified individually.

Pinning stickers

Instagram stickers are really cool dynamic graphics that can be added to your image video Stories to make them more exciting and interesting. A pinned sticker follows a moving element on your video. For example, if you have a video of someone walking, you can have some text above the person's head, moving with them as they walk.

Pinning a sticker to your Story is easy – when you've finished recording your video, swipe up from the bottom of your screen to bring up the stickers. Pick the emoji, GIF or text you want and tap on it to overlay on your video. Next just tap and hold on your chosen sticker, and then release. Two options will appear along the bottom, **Cancel** or **Pin.** A slider will also appear. Use the slider to reach the point in your video where you want to pin your sticker and tap **Pin** to lock it in place in this spot.

When your video plays, the pin will move with your pinned subject! This can take a few attempts to look right but is extremely rewarding if you manage to pin perfectly.

Reveal a new post in your Story

More people view Instagram Stories (swiping left) than view posts (scrolling down). So, when you create a new post it's a good idea to add it to your Story to let the Insta world know about it! Add an element of mystery to get people to visit your profile and view the post by sharing the post in your Story, and then covering most of it with a GIF or Sticker. You can choose a title you like e.g. 'New post, check it out!'

To share a post to your Story, tap the paper plane icon below the photo or video in your feed. Tap **Add Post to Your Story**. To cover it with a GIF or Sticker, click the sticker icon at the top and then scroll to choose a sticker or GIF.

Splitting a video to fit in your Stories

Fifteen seconds goes by very quickly indeed and, as you start creating your Stories, you might find it is difficult to show anything meaningful in such a short time frame. One way to combat this is to break up your longer videos into smaller digestible clips. Instagram splits the first minute of your video into 15-second segments automatically.

For anything longer than a minute, you need an app. There are many apps, most of which are paid for, that allow you to do this. I use **CutStory**. You can search your app store for 'split videos for Instagram'. I would suggest choosing an app that has a high user rating.

Welcome   Services   Products   Our Location   Reviews   Our Team

Adding to your highlights

Occasionally, you may create a Story that's so good or relevant to future visitors, you don't want it to disappear after 24 hours. Fortunately, it doesn't have to. Instagram Stories Highlights are a carefully curated selection of your best Stories that can live on your profile permanently, meaning that your followers can watch them any time they like.

Highlights are located just beneath your profile bio and above your feed, allowing you to showcase the content you want your followers to see first. The beauty of highlights is that the 'best' of your Stories get to stay on your profile under highlights – perfect for new visitors to access at any time. I would like more businesses to try having a 'Welcome' highlight. This could be a Story welcoming new customers in under 30 seconds – consider it your elevator pitch!

Adding to your highlights is simple. First, you'll need to turn on your auto-archive feature to save your stories. Head to your profile screen and open your **Settings**, choose **Privacy**, followed by **Story**. Next, you need to turn on the setting **Save to archive**. You may find this is already turned on. Once you've done this, all your Stories should automatically save to your archive.

Once your archive is set up and you've started saving some Stories, you can pick which ones you want to highlight. On your Instagram profile, click on the white circle with the + sign, named **Highlight**. Now you can choose which Stories you'd like to include.

Finally, give it a title and pick a cover image. You can use a thumbnail from any of your stories or upload a new image. Try to choose a picture that best represents you and your brand, which is aesthetically consistent with the rest of your feed. Tap **Add** to complete the process.

Adding music

Instagram has very kindly obtained permission to use a whole host of popular songs, so you don't need to worry about licensing. You can also display lyrics along with the songs on your Stories. Music stickers with lyrics are only in available regions where music stickers are supported.

Adding music is easy. Once you've created your Story, tap on the sticker icon at the top of the screen and choose **MUSIC** (If you cannot see the music sticker, try updating your app from the app store). From here you'll be able to search for tracks by popularity, mood, and genre. You can also search for a specific song title or artist – just bear in mind that not every song in the world will be on here.

Because Stories are only 15 seconds long, you'll now need to choose which snippet of music you want to use. Think about what will best suit your Story. Do the chorus lyrics enhance what you're trying to tell your followers? Or, perhaps an instrumental piece adds the perfect vibe? Once you've chosen the track you want to use, a new window will open where you can hold and drag the box along the song's timeline until you've reached the section you want to use. Once you're happy, simply tap on **Done** and this will add the music sticker. You can play around with the size and placement of the sticker and, when you're ready to share, just tap on **Send to**.

In Stories, tap followed by

IGTV

IGTV, short for Instagram TV, is a standalone video application by Instagram. It allows for longer videos compared to Instagram. Whilst you can share up to minute-long videos on your own feed, IGTV allows you to upload videos of up to 10 minutes. For larger accounts and verified accounts, you can upload up to 60-minute videos, although these will need to be uploaded from a computer. This feature is an absolute game-changer for brands. It's easy to find – just look for the little television screen in the top right-hand corner and click on that.

The beauty of IGTV is that you can create your own channel – a little bit like YouTube, where you can keep all of your videos in one place for your followers to find. Lengthier content may be a full tour around your premises, a full explanation of the services you offer or a longer client testimonial. Having your videos on their own personalised 'TV channel' helps to keep your brand in the public eye and serves as a reminder for followers who planned to get in contact with you.

Another great way to encourage repeat engagement is to have a recurring 'show' on your channel. Perhaps you have a list of top tips relating to your industry you'd like to share with your followers. Publishing a new tip each week on a regular schedule will get your audience accustomed to coming back and watching your show on your IGTV channel.

Visit your app store to download and install IGTV. After installation, login with your Instagram login details. This will allow you to connect your IGTV channel to your Instagram account.

Polls, questions, love rating, quizzes and more!

One way to get feedback and information from your followers and customers is to simply ask them. Instagram allows you to do this in several ways, such as polls and quizzes and, the best thing is, it's really easy to do.

The poll feature is only available for Stories at present. When your Story is ready to upload, and you've finished adding any text, emojis, hashtags, etc, tap on the sticker Icon at the top of your Story screen and select the **POLL** sticker option. You will then be given the option to type in a yes/no question for your followers to answer.

Once you've added your question, click on **Done** in the top right corner of your screen. Your poll will then appear over your Story and, like a normal sticker, you can make it larger or smaller by pinching the screen, and dragging it into your preferred position.

Once your Story is live, viewers scrolling through Stories will be able to vote on your poll.

You can follow the steps above for a range of other quizzes and questions, including Instagram's emoji slider. This is a fabulous and fun feature that lets your followers answer questions on a sliding scale using emojis instead of numbers.

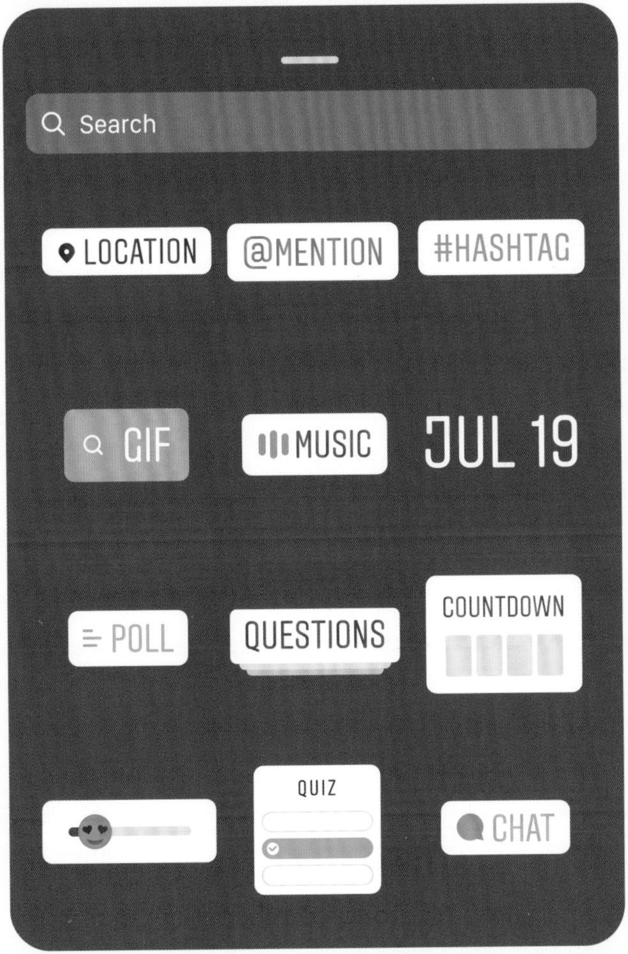
Search
LOCATION
@MENTION
#HASHTAG
GIF
MUSIC
JUL 19
POLL
QUESTIONS
COUNTDOWN
QUIZ
CHAT

Asking your audience a question

Asking questions – or running polls – is a fantastic way to engage with your audience in your Stories. I have always found polls work really well. The Instagram interface makes it incredibly easy for your audience to partake.

When you wish to ask a question, start a Story and click the sticker icon in the top and tap **Questions** or **Poll**. Complete the question you want to ask and share the Story by clicking **Your story**. Poll restricts your audience's answer to Yes or No, whereas Questions are more open-ended.

Ask me a question

Type something...

In Stories, tap  followed by QUESTIONS

Opening Launch

Swipe up now
to book your place
Limited spots available!

**Enjoy one-time amazing launch
offers on the day!**

How do people get the swipe up feature on their Stories?

The swipe up feature on Instagram Stories is a powerful tool for business accounts because it allows you to add a new clickable link to a post, which is different from the link in your bio. You'll need more than 10,000 followers to access this feature but, if you do have a large following like this, then you definitely need to take advantage of the ability to direct your viewers to any specific website page you choose.

To add your link, simply follow the process of uploading a Story (**See page 219 on Starting a Story**) next tap on the link icon on the top right-hand side of your screen. A new window will appear allowing you to paste in a URL. Once you're done, simply tap on the green check-mark (for Android users) or **Done** (for iOS users) to save the link.

You'll now be able to see that your image has been linked, with the hyperlink in the top right-hand corner now white.

Mental health
continued

Social media platforms can be toxic environments and, whether it's a sarcastic or flippant reply to a post or a direct comment that feels personal unless viewed as constructive criticism, I always suggest deleting, blocking and moving on.

Social media can also create in us an unhealthy addiction and fuel our insecurities. The fear of missing out – or FOMO, as it is more commonly known – is a very real threat to our general happiness. Best described as an all-consuming feeling of anxiety and inferiority, we compare our lives unfavourably with those 'perfect' online versions. These are, of course, skewed views that are mostly unfounded and we should all take stock of what matters as well as what is really real and what is 'Instagram' real.

There are a number of positive steps we can take to protect ourselves from the critics (our inner demons as well as other people) and it is important that we are ever mindful of the way we react to social media – and that, at worst, it can sometimes be a cognitive distortion.

Dr. Mahrukh Khwaja is the founder of Mind Ninja, an initiative that, among other things, aims to raise awareness of the importance of mental wellness within professional communities. Dually qualified in Dentistry and Psychology, Mahrukh is also an accredited mindfulness teacher and offers educational service for dental professionals via workshops that are led by a team of experts in healthcare and focus on strengthening emotional resilience.

As an advocate of a healthy online community, she encourages professionals to consider more positive ways to engage using social media.

Mahrukh recognises that the way some industries are marketed on social media can impact negatively on fellow professionals. The beauty of Instagram is the ability to post the 'perfect shot', the very best results and the most flattering angles without any reference to the failures or hours of hard work required to achieve those results. She says: "When we scroll through posts on Instagram and come across an image of something related to our profession we judge ourselves against it and can find ourselves feeling as though we're coming up short, with thoughts like 'I'm not good enough or I'm a failure' "

These knee-jerk reactions, often cognitive distortions of the facts, lead us to catastrophise the situation, bringing to the fore our harsh inner critic and feeding that unforgiving perfectionism with which many business owners are often burdened. With this comes a dread of failure and we may also suffer imposter syndrome – a very real fear that we will be found out as a fraud, a trait far more common among women than men.

She says: 'As with all networks, social media can impact negatively on the confidence of even the thickest-skinned individual, in any industry. For someone who is very active on social media, I feel that it is important to remind myself that the perfectly curated posts are not a reflection of reality and do not show the failures or the complete journey. Regularly reflecting on our own inner narrative helps. We do not need to get lost in feelings of inadequacy.

From an evolutionary perspective, our brain has developed to be highly attuned to stress but, as Mahrukh wryly observes, where once the stressor was a sabre-tooth tiger, perhaps, it is now far more likely to be social media.

She explains: 'These little stressors add up and, if not kept in check, our 'chimp' brain (amygdala) hijacks our responses to a default position of 'flight, fight or freeze'. Although necessary for certain circumstances, the chimp – when untamed – can lead to chronic stress and burnout.

'In terms of social media, the scrolling feature of Instagram, for example, doesn't help the situation, neither does the dopamine hit we get each time we clock up a 'like' on our own posts.

'We all need to be mindful of these thinking distortions and challenge our automatic thoughts when using social media. We should remind ourselves that perfectionism does not exist and that we don't know the failures behind what we often see on Instagram.'

How to enjoy social media 100% of the time

- Limit the platforms you visit to those most effective for your own marketing purposes. It is easy to become overwhelmed with the 'noise' of social media if we are constantly flitting from one platform to another.

- Schedule specific times to check social media or set a timer to limit yourself to 20-30 minutes. For the addicts among us, there are a number of apps that block social media and limit the time we spend scrolling. Check out apps like Offtime, Moment and Flipd.

- Remember that you only ever see the highlights of people's lives. Their posts are not representative of everyday living.

- Hook up with other professionals with whom you engage online to discuss the challenges of the profession, share ideas and experiences or just to grab some downtime. Live life in the real world as much as in the digital.

- Be selective in who you follow. If necessary, unfollow accounts that get you down. The funny memes and inspirational posts can be uplifting on those bad days that we all have!

- Celebrate other people's successes by sharing their posts. As Mahrukh suggests, an ethos of lifting others rather than competing against each other in a battle of egos helps to create a far more supportive business community.

- And lastly, enjoy your marketing endeavours. This book is designed to illustrate just how easy it is to use Instagram as a tool to reach and engage with clients and customers – and demonstrate that it can also be enormously creative and fun!

Get inspired

The accounts on this page demonstrate ways in which you can engage with and capture your audience's attention. These accounts can be used for inspiration, regardless of your industry.

Bakery
- @crosstowndoughnuts
  @pophamsbakery
- @frances_quinn
- @lily_vanilli_cake
  @pollenbakery

Bloggers
@theseptemberchronicles
@the_lois_edit
@theultimatefoodies
@george_in_london
@millykr

Café
- @sketchlondon
- @farmgirlcafe
- @peggyporschenofficial
- @elan_cafe
- @grind

Fitness
@london_fitness_guy
- @zannavandijk
- @bradleysimmonds
- @mattroberts_lifestyle
- @shaunstafford
- @ainsley

Food
@arcadelondon
@gourmet_guy
@ldncheapeats
@lovearchies
@zoukteabar

Health and Medical
@menopause_doctor
- @thefoodmedic
- @drchatterjee
- @gynaegeek
- @doctors_kitchen

Photography
- @davidlloyd ✓
- @fashion_calvin
- @petra____rr
- @thelittleplantation

Real Estate
- @savills ✓
- @investinlondon
- @daniel_daggers

Retail
- @fox_and_weave
- @retold_vintage
- @candylane.co.uk
- @coconutbowls ✓
- @bloomandwild ✓
- @notonthehighstreet ✓

Travel
- @postcardsbyhannah
- @alongdustyroads
- @twins_that_travel ✓
- @livpurvis ✓

Weddings and Events
- @pocketfulofdreams
- @rhubarb_food
- @thelittlelendingco
- @onestylishdayuk
- @katrinaotterwed

Miscellaneous
- @yossi_fisher
- @spark_joy_london
- @amacreator
- @chetnamakan ✓
- @nadinebaggott ✓
- @mad_about_the_house ✓
- @lydiamillenhome

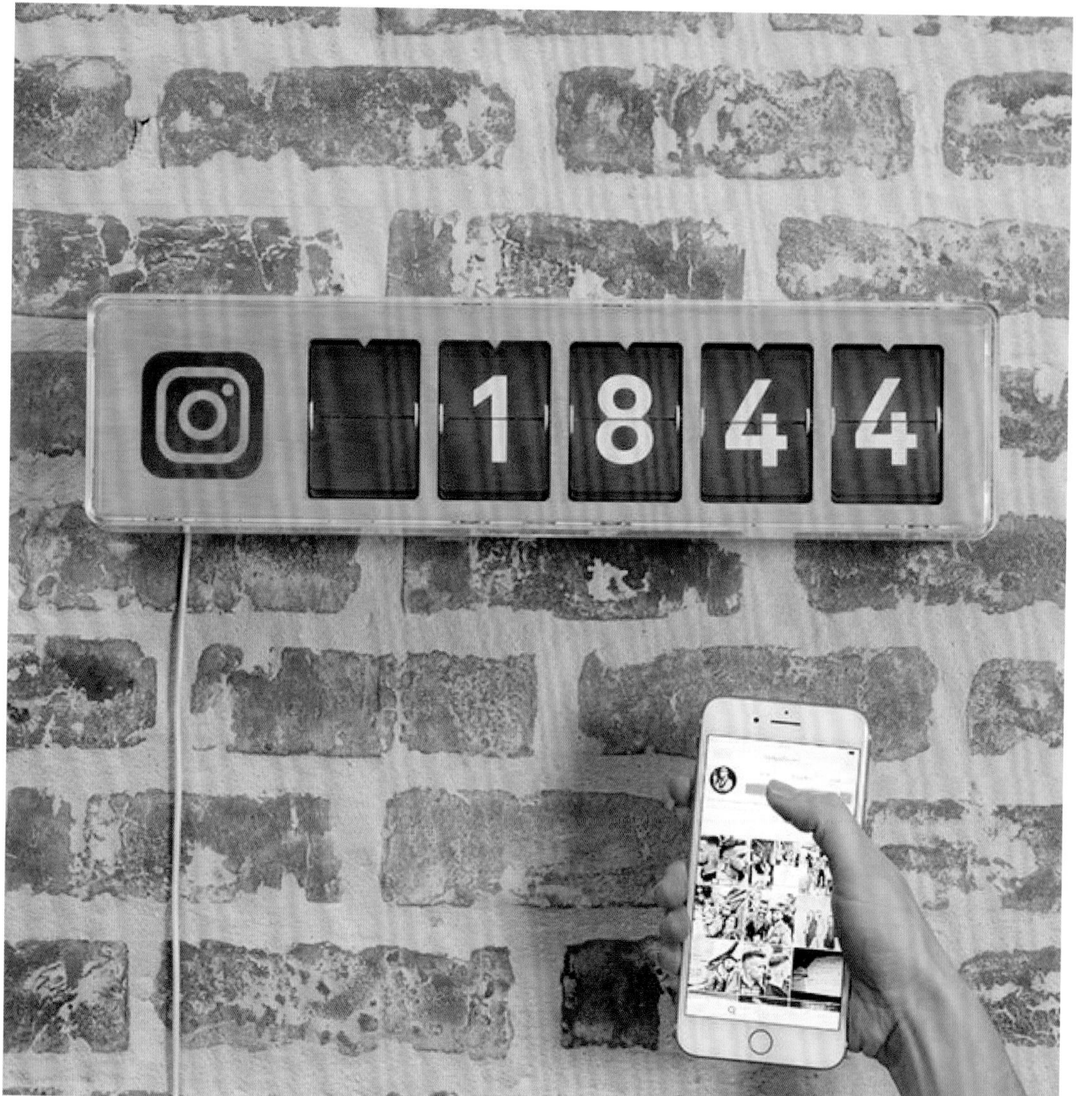
1844

Smiirl

Reaching a high number of followers on Instagram can be a cause for celebration. It shows that you've been managing your profile well and are engaging with new potential customers. But what about the people who don't use social media or who don't follow you? How will they know how popular you are online? That's where Smiirl comes in!

Smiirl is a physical 'counter' that connects to your Instagram account, showing anyone who comes into your place of business just how many followers you have online. Not only is it a visual prompt for them to start following you on Instagram, but it's also a fun way to reinforce your brand strength. Plus you can watch your followers grow in real-time without having to look at your phone! Follow **@smiirl** to learn more.

Recommended apps

To help you supercharge your Instagram account, I've put together a selection of Instagram-related apps for you to explore. Visit your app store to download, and trial any of these apps. Many of these apps are paid apps.

Design / Scheduling
PLANN
PLANOLY
Preview: Planner for Instagram
Layout from Instagram
Highlight Cover Maker
Mojo Story Maker
StoryArt
Later

Video Editing
inShot
Adobe Premiere Rush for Video
KineMaster
CutStory for Instagram Stories

Image Editing
Polarr Photo Editor
VSCO
PicsArt Photo Editor
Snapseed
Afterlight 2
Canva
Photoshop Express
Instaquote
Over
Fontcandy

General
IGTV
Hyperlapse from Instagram
Boomerang from Instagram
Repost: For Instagram
ColorNote
Evernote

Sizing and specifications

Instagram feed   60 seconds

Instagram Stories   15 seconds

Instagram TV (IGTV)   10 minutes

Instagram profile picture size   110px x 110px

Instagram square post size   1080px x 1080px

Instagram landscape size   1080px x 566px

Instagram portrait size   1080px x 1350px

IGTV videos can be both vertical and horizontal

Vertical   Maximum aspect ratio 9:16 and minimum of 4:5

Horizontal   Maximum 16:9 and minimum 5:4

IGTV cover photo   1:1.55 or 420px x 654px

Note, there are several accepted variations of the above.

Please help me improve this book

I knew the moment I released this book, it would immediately date because, of course, the digital world is an exciting one that is forever changing. I want to ensure the next edition is even better with your help. Please scan the QR code below or visit **instaforbusiness.co.uk/feedback** and let me know if you have any feedback, suggestions or improvements for any chapter. Thank you in advance!

Glossary

Instagram Handle This is another term for your account/username, e.g. @bobsbutchers

Visitor Someone who 'visits' your Instagram profile page

Follower This is another Instagram user that follows your account and sees your content within their feed

Following This is the number of followers an account has

Feed This is the page on Instagram where you will see all the posts and images shared by the accounts that you follow

Post This refers to any image or video uploaded to Instagram

Influencer Someone who has the authority to influence a sizeable audience. Often an individual who has a following in a particular niche, which they actively engage with

DM Abbreviation for 'Direct Message'

Profile This is your Instagram account information including name and username, profile photo or logo, bio, and your posts

Insta An abbreviated term for Instagram

The Gram An abbreviated term for Instagram

Hashtag This is the '#' symbol placed in front of a keyword or phrase, which then makes them searchable within Instagram

IG This is an acronym for Instagram

Filter This is a visual effect that can be applied to both photo and video to alter the colours and vibrancy

Blue Tick A blue tick next to an account name means that they have been verified by Instagram and confirmed as an authentic public figure, celebrity or global brand

App Abbreviation for 'Application' which is a software application that you download to your smartphone for access to Instagram

shaz.memon

shaz.memon

I dedicate this book to my daughter. xxx

#daddysprincess

Will you do me a favour?

If you enjoyed reading **Instagram for Business**, would you mind taking a minute to write a review on Amazon? Even a short review helps, and <u>it would mean a lot to me</u>!

Sharing is caring!
If you know anyone that would benefit from any of the advice in this book, please send him or her a copy of this book. It's a great gift to receive :)

Bulk orders
If you would like to place an order of 20 books or more for your group, academy or network, then please visit **www.instaforbusiness.co.uk/trade**

Free updates
I implore you to subscribe to my list to get free updates to this book, bonus materials, and updates on my future projects. Visit **instaforbusiness.co.uk/updates** to subscribe.

Get tagging!
Please tag me in photos and videos of your copy of this book:
@shaz.memon, it would make my day!

Support
Follow **@wells.on.wheels** to see the great work we are doing in rural India. 10 percent of the proceeds from the sale of this book will go to W.O.W.

Thank you for reading and your support!